GAMPOPA'S MAHAMUDRA

THE FIVE-PART MAHAMUDRA OF THE KAGYUS

WITH TEXTS OF THE THROPHU, DRIGUNG,
DRUKPA, AND KARMA KAGYU LINEAGES
AND ORAL COMMENTARY BY
BENCHEN TENGA RINPOCHE

BY TONY DUFF
PADMA KARPO TRANSLATION COMMITTEE

Lydian and Jansen typefaces used throughout.

First edition 10th June, 2008
Second edition March, 2020
ISBN Paper 978-9937-206-07-5
ISBN E-book 978-9937-572-24-8

Produced and Published by
Padma Karpo Translation Committee
Ely, Minnesota
U.S.A.

Committee members for this book: cover design, book layout and typesetting, and translation, Tony Duff.

Web-sites and e-mail contact through:
http://www.pktc.org/pktc
https://www.pktcshop.com
or search Padma Karpo Translation Committee on the web.

Contents

Introduction

"Five-Part Mahamudra" is a specific way of practising Mahamudra that is used in the Kagyu lineage of Tibetan Buddhism. It was first taught by Gampopa to his disciples and since then has become one of the main ways that Mahamudra is practised in the Kagyu lineage. This book presents the teaching and system of instruction that goes with it through the actual Tibetan sources consisting of texts and a commentary. I gathered these materials by hearing the teachings personally then translated and arranged them with helpful background material.

1. THE SOURCE OF THE TEACHING

The Kagyu lineage traces itself back to the Indian siddha Tailopa (also known as Tilopa, Telopa, and Tailopa in Tibetan). His instructions on the practice of the Vajra Vehicle, including the instructions on Mahamudra, went successively to Naropa in India and then to Marpa, Milarepa, and Gampopa in Tibet all of whom are regarded as the early masters of the lineage.

Gampopa [1079–1153 C.E.] represents a pivotal point in the spread of the Kagyu system of teaching and practice. Before him, there had been very little in the way of organized institutions and very little of the teaching had been written down. Starting in his time, institutions developed and the teachings began to be recorded in writing. Gampopa and his gurus are in many ways like the solid trunk of a tree that has not branched out yet. Gampopa is the point on the trunk where myriads of branches appear and the whole turns into a great and luxurious tree.

Gampopa had three heart sons of the secret mantra teachings called "The Three Men from Kham". One was "Grey-Hair" who later became known as the first Karmapa, Dusum Khyenpa. He became the source of the Karma Kamtsang—also known as Karma Kagyu—lineage, which is one of the four lineages, called the Four Greater Lineages of the Kagyu, that developed directly from Gampopa. Another one was Khampa Dorgyal who was also known as Phagmo Drupa. He became the source of the Phagdru (the standard Tibetan abbreviation for Phagmo Drupa) Kagyu lineage, another one of the Four Greater Lineages. Eight of his heart disciples became the sources of nearly all the other Kagyu lineages, called the Eight Lesser Lineages, of the Kagyu. The third one was Saltong Shogom whose incarnations led a recluse's life for many generations and who was not widely known of in Tibet; he did not give rise to any lineage—his incarnations have become known in recent times as Traleg Rinpoche.

On at least one occasion that is recorded but most likely on many occasions, Gampopa gave instructions to his heart disciple Phagmo Drupa on how to practise Mahamudra in a five-part format. Phagmo Drupa used this five-part format as the framework for his successful practice of Mahamudra.

Phagmo Drupa [1110–1170] was already famous as a great teacher and highly accomplished yogin before he came to Gampopa. However, after gaining great attainment under Gampopa's care, he became a very famous teacher, with many disciples. He was well-known for teaching to vast assemblies and in at least one of them, said to have contained five thousand practitioners of the vajra vehicle, taught the complete instructions of Mahamudra in the five-part format that Gampopa had given him and which he had success-fully used for his own practice. This teaching, which was heard, practised, and passed on by his disciples, became a specific method for doing Mahamudra practice and over time become known as "Five-Part Mahamudra" or simply, "The Five-Parts".

The Five-Part instructions went to all of Phagdru's main disciples and so became a central part of the Eight Lesser lineages of the Kagyu—Drigung, Taklung, Throphu, Drukpa, Martshang, Yelpa, Yazang, and Shugseb—that developed because of them. The teaching also went from them into the Four Greater Lineages—Karma, Barom, Tshalpa, and Phagdru. For example, it went from the founder of the Drigung Kagyu, Jigten Sumgon, into the Karma Kagyu where it was transmitted by the lineage holders of that lineage. In this way, this particular teaching called "The Five-Part Mahamudra" became one of the main ways that the Mahamudra teaching was transmitted in the Kagyu lineages after Gampopa.

2. THE TEACHING

2.1. The Reality Called Mahamudra

What is Mahamudra? It is the name for reality used by a particular group of tantric practitioners in ancient India. It sounds exotic but, if you get down to nuts and bolts, it means "reality", no more and no less.

The word "Mahamudra" is often translated as Great Seal and that is not wrong but it usually does not convey the immediate, over-arching sense of reality that the original term does in Indian language. *The Illuminator Tibetan-English Dictionary* has a clear explanation of the word:

> Ultimate reality in the tantric teachings that first came to
> Tibet was called Maha Ati. This was translated into
> Tibetan with "rdzogs pa chen po" and translates into
> English as Great Completion. In the tantric teachings
> that came to Tibet in the later spread of dharma, ultimate

reality was called Mahamudra. This was translated into Tibetan as "phyag rgya chen po"—in Tibetan, "phyag rgya" is the official translation equivalent for the Sanskrit "mudra" and "chen po" for the Sanskrit "maha"—and this is commonly translated into English as "Great Seal".

The translation "Great Seal" is correct. However, the term really has the sense in Indian language of "The Great Stamp" or even better, "The Great Imprint". In Tibetan, a "phyag rgya" refers to the kind of seal or stamp that is actually impressed upon something, like a wax seal used to seal a letter or a postage stamp that will be placed on a letter. These seals are more than just a seal, they are an *imprint* that both exists upon something and conveys some meaning[1]. Phenomena, just by being phenomena, are automatically subject to reality. They are imprinted with that reality. And it is not just one phenomenon or some phenomena that are connected with and hence imprinted with fundamental reality, rather, every phenomenon that there is is necessarily connected with and hence imprinted with that fundamental reality. Therefore the imprint, stamp, or seal of ultimate reality that phenomena bear is not just any imprint but is the one, "great" imprint that stamps itself on everything. So, when the term Mahamudra is used, it actually conveys the meaning "the great imprint, the one that all phenomena bear". It is the imprint of ultimate reality that everything is stamped with, choicelessly.

The tradition explains the term further. The commentators of the tradition break the term "phyag rgya" down into "phyag" and "rgya" which they connect with "mu" and "dra" respectively of the original Sanskrit "mudra". Then the two are explained to mean wisdom and empti-

---

[1] This is exactly the meaning of the original Sanskrit "mudra" in this case—a sign that is displayed and by being displayed conveys meaning.

ness—and sometimes appearance and empti-
ness—respectively. The "chen po" is still correlated with
"maha" but is now explained as meaning that the two,
wisdom and emptiness or appearance and emptiness are,
and have always been, inseparable. However, this
detailed explanation has to be kept within the basic
meaning of the term, which is, if we say it really in collo-
quial English, "The Great Seal of Reality, which is that
all phenomena inevitably are stamped by the fact of
wisdom and emptiness inseparable".

Why is reality equated with wisdom and emptiness inseparable and
why is that equated with appearance and emptiness inseparable? At
root, the things of the average person's world seem to be solid,
permanent, and one, partless thing. That is the way that mind[2]

---

[2] Throughout this book "mind" translates the Sanskrit "chitta" and its
Tibetan equivalent "sems". This mind, which we could call samsaric
mind, is a complex process of knowing that is comes about based on a
fundamental ignorance of reality. However, there is a type of knowing
that underlies, or you could say is at the core of, samsaric mind and
which does not have that fundamental ignorance of reality. This core
of mind has many names, all given for the purpose of distinguishing it
from samsaric mind, such as "mindness", "nature of mind", "the
innate", and so on. These terms are used throughout the teachings
presented here.

The term "mindness" is heavily used in the Mahamudra teachings.
The "ness" at the end of the term accurately translates the Sanskrit
particle "ta", which has two possible meanings according to Sanskrit
grammar. In "mindness", the "ness" supplies the meaning of something that is the very nature of something else. Thus, "mindness"
refers to the very nature of samsaric mind, which is a completely pure
type of knowing that has none of the faults of samsaric mind. This
mindness is the working basis of the tantric path, which, when it has
all the coverings of samsaric mind removed from it, shines forth as

(continued ...)

takes them to be. When this apparent solidity and so forth is looked into, the things that appeared that way suddenly disappear. They were just fictions being invented by mind that was working in a mistaken kind of way. Reality does not have these fictions in it, for reality is what is, not a mistaken take on it. The absence of these things in reality is called "emptiness". However, there is still something about our existence that presents itself to us. When all the mistaken perceptions are removed, there is still a mind that knows. The Sanskrit word used in a number of Indian religions for this kind of mind, "jñana", literally means "knowing", though the religions using the term always understand it to mean a knowing that is intrinsically present or primordially present in any being. This primordially-present knowing does not know in the way that the ignorant mind does; it knows everything, all-at-once, in direct perception without any need of the elaborations that samsaric mind uses when it knows.

This primordially-present knowing is mostly translated as "wisdom" at the time of writing and that is the term used for it in this book. The term "timeless awareness" is also used but that comes from a mistaken understanding of the Tibetan translation of the Sanskrit "jñana". In fact, it is clearly explained in the tantras that jñana does have time, even if it does not have the time of the three times of past, present, and future used by samsaric mind.

Reality is that all phenomenon that appear are always empty of the mistaken, ignorant, samsaric way of knowing them. These completely pure phenomena as they are called are completely pure because they are known by the primordially-present, un-mistaken knowing that has none of the impurities of the samsaric way of knowing them. Hence, all phenomena are actually the appearances that arise in the wisdom that knows them and, as they arise in that

---

² (... continued)
enlightened mind.

wisdom, always lack the mistaken solidity and so forth that a mistaken mind would see them with. It is not that the phenomena arise and are then known by the wisdom, rather, they arise as part of the energy of the wisdom itself. Thus all phenomena are, you can say, wisdom and emptiness inseparable or appearance and emptiness inseparable; when understood that way, the meaning is the same.

The yogic tradition of ancient India that understood reality in this way called it Mahamudra, the great stamp of reality that all phenomena are always stamped with, and their teaching was that reality is wisdom and emptiness as an inseparable unity.

2.2. The Practice of Mahamudra

It should be clear from the foregoing that the term Mahamudra is a term for reality. Beings need a practice to get back to that reality and the tantric systems that came from India to Tibet contained a number of different practices for that purpose. The tantric teachings that came into the Kagyu tradition included several: the teaching of Mahamudra itself, the teachings of deity practices of various sorts, and the yogic teachings summed up by Naropa into what were called "The Six Teachings of Naropa"—Fierce Heat, Illusory Body, Dreaming, Luminosity, Transference, and Intermediate State. The Mahamudra teaching is directly related to the practice called "Luminosity" contained in the six teachings of Naropa. The practice of Mahamudra is also contained in a teaching called "Sahajayoga" or "Co-emergence Yoga". This latter name is mostly seen in English these days as "Co-emergent Union" but there is a point here: Mahamudra is a term for reality whereas Luminosity and Co-emergence Yoga are names of the practice of that reality. As recorded in *Lord Phagmo Drupa's Interviews*,[3] Phagmo Drupa once asked Gampopa about the two:

> What difference is there, if any, between Mahamudra and Co-emergence Yoga?

Gampopa's reply made it very clear:

> Mahamudra is a timeless reality that is always present, whereas Co-emergence Yoga is a practice that is done at various times and time after time, of uniting non-reality with reality, where reality is expressed above as the four different aspects of a buddha's enlightenment.

How did Gampopa see the teaching and practice of Mahamudra in relation to the other teachings and practices of reality that were handed down to him? His guru, Milarepa, had put strong emphasis on Fierce Heat, so that became a particularly important teaching in the Kagyu from Milarepa's time onwards. The writings in the collected works of Gampopa show that he did teach all of the six teachings of Naropa but preferred to guide his students with the practice of Fierce Heat mixed with Mahamudra where possible and, where not possible, did teach the path of Mahamudra alone as his main way of leading disciples. This is very clear from another interchange between Phagmo Drupa and Gampopa recorded in the same text as just quoted above. Phagmo Drupa asked:

> In terms of practising to gain experience, which is the most profound oral instruction?

Gampopa replied by listing what he had heard other people say to be the most profound instruction for practice. He started with the Kadampa's mind training and went through several others, mentioned deity practice, then arrived at what his guru Milarepa

---

[3] Published by Padma Karpo Translation Committee in *Gampopa Teaches Essence Mahamudra, Interviews with His Heart Disciples, Dusum Khyenpa and Others*, 2011, ISBN: 978-9937-572-08-8.

had said. Having mentioned them all, he then answered the
question:

> ... I heard Guru Mila say, "The wind-based practice of
> Fierce Heat is the profound meditation".
>
> Adding it all up, for any given person, the dharma in
> which a person develops certainty is the profound one.
> So, for me, if you devote yourself to the guru and medi-
> tate on pairing Fierce Heat with Mahamudra and so train
> your mind in the enlightenment mind,[4] since both your
> own and others' aims will happen at the same time be-
> cause of it, this is the profound one.

Phagmo Drupa queried:

> Well then, do you prefer to lead people through Fierce
> Heat to start with or through Mahamudra?

The reply came:

> It depends on the person's type. Younger people with
> good physical elements and channels who are instructed
> in and meditate on Fierce Heat itself will quickly develop
> the signs of progress. Then, if they are given Mahamu-
> dra, experience and realization will quickly dawn. For
> older people who are in the category of not being able to
> tune the winds, I prefer to give Mahamudra or Co-emer-
> gence Yoga, though there is the possibility that, if Maha-
> mudra is not produced within the mindstream, they

---

[4] Skt. bodhichitta, Tib. byang chub sems. "Enlightenment mind" is
the exact translation of "bodhichitta". Note that this is not the same
as "mind for enlightenment". "Bodhichitta" means the actual enlightenment mind all the way from its being totally covered up in a sentient
being to its being totally uncovered in a buddha. The term "enlightenment mind" is used throughout this book simply because it says
much more to English speakers.

might fall into bad activities and develop a very jaded and problematic character.

These interchanges are from an early, possibly initial, meeting between Gampopa and Phagmo Drupa. Phagmo Drupa asked a lot of questions of Gampopa, obviously to get a sense of Gampopa's style and knowledge. Later, after the required phase of testing the prospective guru, Phagmo Drupa decided to become a disciple of Gampopa.

At one point Phagmo Drupa returned to Gampopa who was staying in his hermitage in Gampo Valley, and, with some other yogins, asked for an introduction to the nature of mind[5]. Now, in this meeting, he was asking for the actual instructions needed for practice. Gampopa gave a very pithy answer that the reality of mind is none other than the dharmata of a buddha's mind[6] and went on to say that, if someone wants to get to that state of being, he has to go to an isolated place and practice. Gampopa then mentioned a sequence of things that have to be done for the practice: things prior to the actual practice of Mahamudra; the actual practice of Mahamudra—the Co-emergent Yoga, as passed down through Tailo, Naro; and so on.

Having done that, Gampopa instructed Phagmo Drupa and the others to go to an isolated place suitable for practice and practice in sessions consisting of five parts. This part of the interchange

---

[5] See the glossary for "introduce" and "introduction". It is the standard term used in ordinary life when one person introduces another person to a third person or thing that they have not met before or do not remember. The term is also used in the Vajra Vehicle in exactly the same way it is used in ordinary life, but is used to indicate that the guru gives the disciple an introduction to his or her own mindness.

[6] "Dharmata" means the innate quality of something, what it is really like. For example, the dharmata of water is wetness. See the glossary for more.

became the source of the whole Five-Part Mahamudra teaching that has become a mainstay of Kagyu practice. Accordingly, the full text of that interchange is presented at the beginning of the book following this introduction.

2.3. The Specific Practice of Mahamudra Done in Five Parts

Luminosity of the Six Teachings of Naropa and of Co-emergence Yoga are distinct teachings of Mahamudra that were part of the transmission of the tantric teachings that came from India to Tibet. Five-Part Mahamudra was not another teaching that was transmitted with them. Rather, Five-Part Mahamudra is Gampopa's instruction on how to do an effective session of Mahamudra practice. Gampopa gave an explanation of Mahamudra following the co-emergence system that came down through Shantipa to Tailopa and thence down to Gampopa as explained before. He then instructed his disciples to do the practice of Mahamudra in sessions with five parts to them, so that they could conduct a complete and effective session of Mahamudra practice.

Although these instructions originated with Gampopa, Phagmo Drupa was the heart disciple who heard and practised the five-part instruction and gained realization through it. Historically, Phagmo Drupa was the one who taught this style of practice to others and who became well known in the Kagyu as the source of this teaching, even though the teaching originated with Gampopa.

It has been recorded that Phagmo Drupa summed up the five parts and taught them to one large congregation in these words:

> First, meditate on enlightenment mind;
> Meditate on the yidam deity;
> Meditate on the holy guru;
> Meditate on Mahamudra;
> Afterwards, seal it with dedication.

Thus, a session of Five-Part Mahamudra begins with the development of enlightenment mind. This, which necessarily includes
taking refuge, means that the essential points of the practice of the
Lesser and Great Vehicles are included in a session. It is followed
by meditation on oneself as the personal deity, which means that
the creation stage practice of secret mantra is fully included in the
session. That is followed by guru-yoga, unification with the guru's
enlightened being, which means that a session includes one of the
greatest key points of secret mantra, devotion to the guru. It
arouses and intensifies devotion, which is one of the main forces
behind actually being able to join with the guru's being and experience the reality of Mahamudra because of it. It gives the greatest
possibility that the next part, which is the practice of Mahamudra
itself, will be effective. The fourth part is the main practice,
Mahamudra. Mahamudra corresponds to the completion stage of
practice of secret mantra so, by practising Mahamudra, both
creation and completion stages of secret mantra are included in the
session. Once that has been done, the session needs to be sealed
and closed properly, which is done according to the Buddha's
general instructions for all types of meditation, with dedication. In
that way, the actual practice of Mahamudra, which is one of the
core teachings of the Kagyu, is couched within a framework of
other practices that create the best environment for doing the
practice, and that is the point of Five-Part Mahamudra.

3. THE TEXTS AND COMMENTARY
PRESENTED HERE

The teaching on Mahamudra itself is primarily an oral teaching
passed on, usually to a limited audience, for the sake of the listener's
practice and realization. However, the teaching has been recorded
in writing at times and these writings are often used as a basis for
explaining the practice. This book consists of a variety of writings
of Kagyu masters that show the Five-Part Mahamudra teaching
from its beginnings with Gampopa and Phagdru down through its

transmission through the various Kagyu lineages and ending with a complete commentary on one of the texts given by a principal, present-day holder of the lineage.

A number of books on Mahamudra have been published in the West. However, most of them have been transcripts of a specific teaching given by a specific teacher or a translation of a single text. While these sorts of publications have many merits, they do not open readers up to the extraordinary vistas of Tibetan dharma literature. There are a couple of books on Five-Part Mahamudra but they come from the perspective of one lineage and fulfill the time-honoured need for presenting the teaching just of that lineage. They do not provide the opportunity to see how the teaching developed and how differing teachers had their own ways of presenting the teaching while always maintaining the core teaching.

Therefore, although this book is like others in that it contains a translation of an oral teaching by a great teacher of the tradition and a translation of the text being commented on, it goes a step further. It also offers a view of the whole subject as presented by the great authors of not one but several Kagyu lineages and during not one time but across many centuries. The rest of the introduction sets out these various authors.

As mentioned earlier, the main part of this book starts with the exchange between Gampopa and Phagdru that resulted in the whole teaching called Five-Part Mahamudra. This comes from a text called *Phagmo Drupa's Interviews*, which is one of the texts preserved within *Gampopa's Collected Works*. I used the Derge Edition of Gampopa's *Collected Works* for this text.

That is followed by a text written by a direct disciple of Phagmo Drupa called The Translator from Throphu. This disciple was the source of the Throphu Kagyu and his text was written nearly one thousand years ago, in the 1100's, right at the beginning of the Kagyu lineage. The text has a pithy, direct, no-frills presentation of Phagmo Drupa's original teaching and this is very much the style of the early Kagyu. The energy and flavour of a Kagyu yogin doing nothing but a Kagyu yogin's practice comes through very clearly.

That is followed by the teaching of Drigung Kyobpa, another direct disciple of Phagmo Drupa. His teaching also is a very pithy one and again reflects the no-nonsense, get-down-to-it style of the early Kagyu. Drigung Kyobpa's original words come to us arranged within a larger commentary written in the mid-1500's. This part of the commentary is more sophisticated in its presentation, putting more framework around the original teaching. However, the style of the commentary still has a strong sense of practice lineage, which is not surprising given that the author, Zhamar Konchog Yanlag, was very well known for his excellent practice. This text comes with a complete oral commentary by the present-day Karma Kagyu lineage holder, Benchen Tenga Rinpoche. Although his commentary is not exhaustive, it is sufficient to make the meaning clear, and certainly provides a good basis for anyone wanting to go further with the practice.

The third text was also written in the mid-1500's and very clearly shows the style that had developed in Tibetan literature by then of a much more ordered composition, with sections and sub-sections inserted throughout the text and a lot more information provided in general. This text is from Padma Karpo, the fourth Drukchen, that is, the fourth head of the Drukpa Kagyu.

Finally, there is a text from the eighth Situ Rinpoche that was written at the height of the renaissance of Buddhadharma that occurred in Tibet in the 1700's. He too was a great scholar and sometimes was called "all-knowing" like Padma Karpo. However, unlike Padma Karpo, he is known as a key figure in that revival; he was a brilliant scholar whose ways and works made him into one of the leading renaissance figures of his time. He was a masterful scholar and expositor and this is the feeling that comes through in his text.

3.1. A Text From the Throphu Kagyu

Phagmo Drupa's disciple called Rinpoche Gyaltsa and his disciple called "The Translator from Throphu, Nub Jampay Pal" [1173–1225] are, together, the source of the Throphu Kagyu which is one of the Eight Lesser Lineages of the Kagyu. Nub Jampay Pal settled in Throphu, a place in Tsang, and established a monastery there. His talks were written down and one text of those instructions he had heard, called *One Hundred Foremost instructions*[7], contained the teaching on the Five-Part Mahamudra. The oral instructions and writings that went with them were kept by the lineage.

The Throphu Kagyu was a very small lineage and its teachings mostly ended up in other Kagyu lineages. As time went by, some of these teachings were either lost or in danger of loss. In the mid-nineteenth century, Jamgon Kongtrul Lodro Thaye went around Tibet collecting these various oral lineages of Kagyu teaching that were in danger of being lost and the texts that went with them. He published the texts in a major collection called *The Treasury of Oral*

---

[7] Foremost instruction is one of several types of oral instruction. The importance of this type of oral instruction can be understood from Situ Chokyi Jungnay's text. He says that the instructions used to impart the realization of Mahamudra to students cannot be just any type of oral instruction but must be the type that is "an experiential kind of instruction ... which are not mere ornaments to the word of the Conqueror". With this, he is saying that foremost instruction is not the usual type of oral instruction used to clarify the words of the Buddha (and other great teachers) that operate simply by adding more to the meaning till it is clear; it is much more than that. Foremost instruction is a special type of instruction that incorporates the power of personal experience and realization of either the teacher himself or the teacher's teachers. These words are usually kept very private and, because of that, have a lot of power when they are used, much more so than ordinary types of oral instruction. See the glossary for more.

Instructions and used that as a basis for passing on the transmissions of these instructions so that they would not be lost. The Throphu Five-Part Mahamudra in the larger collection mentioned above was extracted and included in the *Treasury of Oral Instructions*. The extracted text was called "A Written Instruction Coming from the Throphu Kagyu on the Five-Part Mahamudra". The original text was probably just entitled "Five-Part Mahamudra" but the name would have been changed to indicate where the text came from, a standard procedure in Tibetan literature.

The text is short, with a very clear statement of the five parts. It gives a sense of the pithiness of the instructions that were passed on by Phagmo Drupa to his disciples and the early, very down-to-earth Kagyu style. One result of that is that the message that these are instructions for practice comes through very clearly. This quality is very much the hallmark of the Kagyu lineage, especially in the earlier days of its transmission in Tibet, as exemplified in the songs and stories of Milarepa. As the centuries went by in Tibet, earlier instructions that were often very simple in content became embellished with the frills of words and explanations. The instructions in this text do not have that kind of elaboration. Instead, they just show the basic message of what is to be practised.

3.2. A Text Based on the Teachings of the Drigung Kagyu

A much stronger lineage of the Five-Part Mahamudra teaching came through Phagmo Drupa's heart-disciple Rinchen Pal [1143–1217] who also became very famous in Tibet for his practice and realization. Rinchen Pal was in the large assembly mentioned earlier that received the five part instruction from Phagmo Drupa. All the stories about him say that he practised these and all the other instructions received from his guru to the point of total proficiency and attained great realization of the Buddha's teachings. After doing so, he established his seat in the place called Drigung. The lineage that developed from him was thus called the Drigung

Kagyu and it is another of the Eight Lesser Lineages of the Kagyu. After attaining realization, he became widely known as Drigung Kyobpa, "Protector of the Drigung" and also as Jigten Sumgon, "The Guardian of the Three Worlds".

Jigten Sumgon transmitted Phagmo Drupa's teaching of the Five-Part Mahamudra verbally to others and at that time added further structure to it. Specifically, he added information on the key points associated with each of the five parts, information that became known as the "Ten Dharmas, Three Dharmas". In regard to this additional information of the Ten Dharmas, Three Dharmas that Jigten Sumgon added to the Five-Part instructions of Phagmo Drupa, a text says,

> The Drigungpa ... accomplished the key points of the practice for each of the five parts. He pacified the obstacles both temporary and ultimate for each of the five parts, and obtained, in full, every one of the supreme and ordinary qualities of accomplishment in the vajra vehicle. In that way, he came to full knowledge of each of the five parts. He then showed every one of all the profound and the vast instructions as its meaning and also showed the "Ten Dharmas, Three Dharmas" as its key points ...

In other words he transmitted the meaning of all the instructions of his guru as the teaching on the five parts and then, on top of that, since he had personally accomplished the key points associated with the practice, taught those key points in what became known as "The Ten Dharmas, Three Dharmas".

The Drigung Kyobpa's specific way of presenting the Five-Part Mahamudra stayed with the Drigung Kagyu but also found its way into the other, greater Kagyu lineages. In particular, it became a part of the Karma Kagyu lineage. The fifth Zhamar of the Karma Kagyu lineage, Konchog Yanlag [1525–1583], who was also known by the epithet "Subject of the Jewels", composed a text as a commentary to the Five-Part Mahamudra as transmitted by the Drigung Kyobpa. Zhamar's commentary consists of a preface followed by five sections of instructions, one for each of the five parts. The preface quotes Phagmo Drupa's words as the basis for the teaching. The instructions for each section were sometimes written by himself but in most cases were assembled from the writings of his predecessors the second Zhamarpa Kacho Wangpo and fourth Zhamarpa Chokyi Drakpa, both of whom were prolific authors. Then these instructions for each section were crowned with a long quote from Drigung Kyobpa that starts with the key points of the topic, called the Ten Dharmas, Three Dharmas, and ends with verses from Phagmo Drupa. As it says in the colophon,

> ... the one called "Subject of the Jewels" put together this ex-pression of just the important parts of the words of the Protector of Beings, Phagmo Drupa, the words of the Protector of the Three Worlds, Drigungpa, the writings of Glorious Khachopa "Introduction to One's Own Mind", and the Chokyi Drakpa Yeshe Palzangpo's, "Instructions on the Five Parts" ...

This text was also included in *The Treasury of Oral Instructions*, one of the five treasuries compiled by the first Jamgon Kongtrul.

3.3. A Complete Oral Commentary By Benchen Tenga Rinpoche

The lineage of this instruction coming from the Jigten Sumgon and passed down to Zhamarpa has been passed down in the Karma Kagyu since then. One of the present-day holders of the teaching is Benchen Tenga Rinpoche, third incarnation of the Tenga Tulku line.

Tenga Rinpoche was born in 1932 in Eastern Tibet. The name of the parents, his birth date, and birthplace were prophesied by the eleventh Situ Rinpoche at the request of the ninth Sangye Nyenpa Rinpoche. Tenga Rinpoche was found at the age of seven, where-upon he began his studies. He took the ordination of a bhikshu at the age of nineteen, and received thorough Buddhist training and education in Benchen and Palpung Monasteries from the ninth Sangye Nyenpa Rinpoche and the former Situ and Jamgon Rinpoches, respectively. He also studied tantric rituals and philosophy with many different masters and learned traditional Tibetan medicine from his uncle. He completed his studies with a three year retreat.

He left Tibet in 1959, after the Communist Chinese invasion, spent one and a half years in Kalimpong, then settled at Rumtek Monastery, the seat of H.H. the sixteenth Karmapa. He served His Holiness for seventeen years, the last nine years of which he acted as Vajra Master of Rumtek. He accompanied His Holiness on his first tour to America and Europe in 1974 and lived next to the great Swayambunath Stupa in Nepal, since 1976 where he founded Benchen Phuntsok Dargyeling Monastery. He also founded a retreat centre in Pharping.

Tenga Rinpoche was one of the grand old masters who received his entire education in Tibet in the old way. He was full of knowledge and realization and very highly regarded in the Tibetan Buddhist tradition in general and within the Karma Kagyu Tradition in particular. In the spring of 2004, Tenga Rinpoche gave a complete explanation of the Five-Part Mahamudra to about one hundred of his students at his monastery in Swayambunath using the text of the fifth Zhamar mentioned immediately above. The long-time servant of the Buddha's dharma, Tony Duff, received the teaching in its entirety and translated the text using Tenga Rinpoche's commentary as a guide, then translated the entire commentary to it.

3.4. A Text from the Drukpa Kagyu

Tsangpa Gyare was another of the heart-sons of Phagmo Drupa. He was a yogin who was not a monk and was remarkable both for his high level of realization and the extraordinary number of students that he was said to have—some put it as high as fifty thousand, which is really an enormous number in the Tibetan system.

One of Tsangpa Gyare's heart disciples was a repa[8] called Lingje Repa. The teaching lineage that came down through them became known as the Drukpa Kagyu which in Tibet was known for practice, even amongst the other Kagyus, who were already known for their emphasis on practice. Correspondingly, it was known for having many realized practitioners. The Drukpa Kagyu has several sub-lineages but the tradition as a whole is considered to be headed by a series of incarnations called the Drukchens.

The Drukchens are regarded as emanations of Tsangpa Gyare and, in line with his reputed high level of realization, are universally considered to be very accomplished masters. More than that though, they are famous for having extraordinary knowledge of dharma and incisive abilities when using that knowledge for the sake of disciples. The greatest scholar amongst them to date has been the fourth Drukchen, Padma Karpo [1527–1592]. He was exceptionally learned, so much so that he was given the title "all-knowing", a title that was bestowed approximately once a century in Tibet when someone of amazing breadth of knowledge appeared. As might be expected of someone with this kind of quality, he was a prolific author with his collected works totalling over twenty volumes.

His treatment of the Five-Part Mahamudra also marks a shift in literary style in Tibet. Note how he arranges the teaching into topics and sub-topics, and adds the teachings on the ordinary and extraordinary preliminaries. The original teaching was very pithy and did not contain these things.

---

[8] Tib. ras pa. A repa was a yogin who wore only a thin cotton cloth called a "re". Repas could do this, even in the extreme cold of the snowy mountains of Tibet, because of their yogic practice that produced warmth in the body.

His text is interesting in two other ways. Firstly, it shows the particular style of the Drukpa Kagyu, who have their own preferences and ways when expounding Mahamudra; there has been little Drukpa Kagyu literature translated till now, so this should be of great interest. Secondly, Padma Karpo is one of the really great authors of Tibet, known to followers of all Tibetan lineages, and has a unique style of writing. He is well known for his erudite compositions which are marked by an extraordinary level of detail woven into a very short space, usually with layer upon layer of meaning in the words. This makes his works difficult to translate without losing meaning and also requires that the reader pay close attention so as to get the fullness of what he is saying. The other texts included here are straightforward to read, if you know the material, but Padma Karpo demands that you stop and think about each sentence and how it joins to the picture that he has been building up. Certainly there will be places in his text where, unless you are very knowledgeable, you could have trouble understanding him.

3.5. A Text from the Karma Kagyu

The final text in this book is from the Karma Kagyu and written by the eighth Situ Rinpoche. In general, the Situ Rinpoche's are one of a group of the four second-highest tulkus of the Karma Kagyu lineage, with the highest being the head of the lineage, Karmapa. The eighth Situ had several names though he is mainly called Great Pandit Situ Chokyi Jungnay in deference to his great knowledge. He lived from 1700 to 1744.

Situ Chokyi Jungnay was one of the key figures in a great revival of Buddhadharma that happened in Tibet in the 1700's. A feature of his writing is sheer brilliance of presentation. Like Padma Karpo, he was very erudite, but reading his writings gives you the feeling of touching gold. Padma Karpo tends to be more breath-taking—when you finally pull all the threads together—where Situ Rinpoche is exceptionally clear and fine, from beginning to end. Situ

Rinpoche's text is appropriately the last one in the book, because his style of presentation and the development of thought in Tibet had reached a pinnacle. Later authors could draw things together or be as erudite but there are no further baubles to be added; everything that could be done has been done, so to speak.

Situ Rinpoche's text demands a good knowledge of dharma, though it should be a little more accessible than Padma Karpo's text. Situ Rinpoche's opening presentation of the five parts and, following that, of the two types of enlightenment mind, are very nicely done. His presentation of the distinctions between shamatha and vipashyana practices of Mahamudra are especially useful. These distinctions are made in the other texts but not as clearly. An interesting point is that his work is entirely in verse but the Tibetan reads more as a continuous piece of prose that has been put into verse. This kind of composition could be the hack job of an incapable author but, in this case, it clearly shows Situ Rinpoche's mastery over words and composition. This text is my favourite in many ways.

4. ABOUT THE TEXTS AND TRANSLATION

There are a number of texts on the five part instruction within the Kagyu lineage. Three of the texts in this book can be found in Jamgon Kongtrul Lodro Thaye's *Treasury of Oral Instructions*. A fourth Five-Part Mahamudra text in that collection called *The Torma Empowerment of the Five-Part Instructions* is a small text by which an empowerment into Mahamudra is given using a torma as the basis for the empowerment. There is also a fifth text by Lorepa, one of the great early yogins of the Drukpa Kagyu, however, there was not space to include it. The text of Padma Karpo is one of his many writings on Mahamudra that can be found in his collected works.

The edition of *The Treasury of Oral Instructions* used as a source for the texts is a modern-day reprint of an earlier edition from Tibet. As is so often the case with Tibetan texts, this edition is known for having a measure of errors in it. Therefore, in order to make the translations for this publication, I edited copies of the texts myself, and in the case of the text transmitting the Drigung Kyobpa's words, H.H. Drigung Kyabgon Rinpoche, the present-day successor to the Drigung Kyobpa, also provided corrections. The text from Padma Karpo was obtained from the Drukpa Kagyu Heritage Project, of which I was the director during the ten years that it functioned in Kathmandu, Nepal.

4.1. About Sanskrit

Sanskrit terminology is properly transliterated into English with the use of diacritical marks. However, these marks often cause discomfort to less scholarly readers and can distance them from the work. The intent here was to publish a book primarily for practitioners, therefore Sanskrit diacriticals have been used only when needed for mantras and when there was Sanskrit in the original Tibetan text. More scholarly types might not be satisfied with this choice and we apologise to them in this time when such issues of translation are still being worked out.

4.2. Further Study

Padma Karpo Translation Committee has amassed a wide range of materials to help those who are studying this and related topics. Please see the chapter "Supports for Study" at the end of the book for all the details.

4.3. What is not Included

The oral instructions always contain special teachings, such as the foremost instructions already mentioned, which are not meant for public display. Thus, this book gives nearly all of the oral instructions passed on by Tenga Rinpoche but two parts were excluded simply because they are not for public display. Anyone who receives these teachings in person will obtain these specific instructions. For example, the details of the deity visualization and practice were not included here but a student would receive them. Similarly, an oral instruction of the guru-yoga visualization that is specific to this lineage was given but is not included here. The complete instructions of Mahamudra are included but the fact is that you cannot practise them until you have received the instructions yourself from a qualified guru. At very least, you must have what is called "the introduction to the nature of mind" to be able to utilize them.

4.4. The Real Point

It is always worth saying that texts like this are not meant for scholarship; they are the absolute meat and potatoes of the path of the Vajra Vehicle. They are meant to be used by a competent guru as a basis for imparting the instructions of the path of Mahamudra orally to the students. The guru uses them as a basis for transmitting the energy of his understanding about the path and the practice in general to the students. Especially though, the guru uses any of a variety of methods, including ones suggested in here in the section on "introduction", to introduce the student directly to the nature of the student's own mind.

When the student has had this kind of introduction and then practised the instructions on what to do with it, the words of experience mentioned above become a key part of discussions of experience and development along the path. Their use by the guru can elevate the student's level of certainty in the nature of mind, enormously.

May you recognize the nature of your mind,
Become certain of it,
And complete the training in it
To be a cornucopia of benefit and ease
For those who have not yet done so!

Tony Duff,
Swayambunath,
Nepal, 2017

PART I

The Source:
Gampopa's Instruction to Phagmo Drupa That Began the Five-part Mahamudra Teaching

Lord Gampopa

Sugata Phagmo Drupa

An Excerpt From
Phagmo Drupa's Interviews With Gampopa

Phagmo Drupa offered:

> Homage to you, precious guru. Guru Jewel, I have fully investigated both samsara and nirvana and request you to give me an introduction to dharmata.

The guru said:

> We speak of the two, "buddhas and sentient beings", so what does that mean? For mind, there are the two ways of knowing, knowing reality directly and not knowing it directly, and these are present in a person as recognizing the direct knowing and not recognizing it respectively. The direct knowing is called "rigpa". If that rigpa is recognized, just that is called "buddhahood", so what is required is that the rigpa has to be introduced as one's own dharmata.[9]

---

[9] As Gampopa says, there are only two sides to existence. There is the side that comes with mind that directly knows reality and the side that comes with mind not directly knowing it—the sides of a buddha's enlightenment and a sentient being's ignorant confusion. The latter is simply a twisted version of the former, so if one wants to go to buddhahood, which is a return to one's dharmata or original quality of
(continued ...)

You go to mountainous areas and so on, congenial places where disenchantment can be produced and experience can develop. There you arouse enlightenment mind thinking, "For the purposes of sentient beings, I will attain buddhahood". You meditate on your body as the deity. You meditate on the guru over your crown. Then, not letting your mind be spoiled with thoughts, not altering this mind—because it is nothing whatsoever—in any way at all, set yourself in illumination which is pure, vividly present, cleaned out, cleared out, and wide-awake![10]

---

[9] (... continued)
being, one has start with an introduction to the mind that knows directly.

"Knowing directly" and "not knowing directly" translate the Sanskrit terms "vidya" and "avidya" and their Tibetan equivalents "rig pa" and "ma rig pa". "Rigpa" is often translated as "awareness" but that is incorrect for various reasons, such as that rigpa is not a passive way of knowing. Then, "ma rig pa" is mostly translated as "ignorance" which is not wrong but fails to make the all-important paired connection with non-ignorance, that is, with rigpa.

[10] The first four of the five parts—arouse enlightenment mind, meditate on the deity, meditate on the guru, and meditate on mahamudra—are shown in this paragraph. Following the introduction to the practice of mahamudra contained in the last sentence, Gampopa goes on to give Phagmo Drupa and the other yogins present a lengthy instruction on mahamudra, which can be read in Padma Karpo Translation Committee's *Gampopa Teaches Essence Mahamudra, Interviews with His Heart Disciples, Dusum Khyenpa and Others*, 2011, ISBN: 978-9937-572-08-8. The fifth part, dedication, is not shown here but is explained later.

The Teaching:
The Instructions of Phagmo Drupa
as Transmitted by
The Translator of Throphu,
Jampay Pal

A Written Instruction
Coming From the Throphu Kagyu
on the Five-Part Mahamudra

I prostrate to the holy gurus.[11]

The introduction in five parts to mahamudra, the essence of the enlightened mind of the great guru Naropa, is as follows:

1) Arousing the mind for supreme enlightenment
2) Meditating on guru-yoga
3) Meditating on the pride of the yidam deity
4) Introducing mindness as buddha
5) Dedicating the roots of merit to complete enlightenment.[12]

---

[11] ... of the Kagyu lineage.

[12] "Introducing" here refers to giving the introduction to mindness. "Mindness" has been explained in the book's introduction; it is one of many terms meaning the nature of mind and it is a path term. "Actuality of mind" is another term for the nature of mind, but it is a ground term, meaning that it is used only when describing the ground situation. It refers to the reality which is the nature of mind as it actually is, regardless of whether one is a practitioner or not, a buddha or not. "Mindness" on the other hand is a path term. It refers to exactly the same thing as "actuality of mind", but does so from the practitioner's

(continued ...)

1) With very strong loving kindness and compassion, you should meditate while repeating from your heart three times the arousing of both aspiring and entering enlightenment minds.

2) During the daytime at the crown of your head and during the night-time in your heart, visualise on a three-fold seat of lion throne, lotus, and moon one atop the other, your root guru with his hands in equipoise mudra and arouse the recognition that he is buddha. Supplicate him intensely.

3) Arouse the pride of your body with its mandala of channels being the yidam deity. You should do one hundred and eight or so recitations.[13]

4) There are two introductions, one to the uncontrived innate and the other to discursive thought as luminosity.

4.1) For the first, with your body set in the postures of meditation and not manipulating your mind, let the present mind be relaxed, still, and all-inclusive. Remove the obstacles of the four points of straying and the three deviations. Allowing the appearances of threefold sinking, agitation, and rational-mind's doings to shine forth within the meditative state removes the obstructions to wisdom waking up of itself via the conditions of sights and sounds.

---

[12] (... continued)
perspective. It conveys the sense to a practitioner that he might still have baggage of dualistic mind that has not been purified yet but there is an innate nature to that mind that he can work with in order to rid himself of the baggage of dualistic mind. When mindness has been fully uncovered, the disciple's mind has become the "dharmakaya" of a buddha, which is a fruition term corresponding to the ground and path terms indicated above.

[13] ... of the deity's mantra.

4.2) For the second, within that state some discursive thought might arise, but by looking nakedly at what has arisen there is nothing to be seen and the discursive thought will go on to self-liberation in just that absence of anything to be seen. Allowing such thoughts to shine forth as appearances that happen due to the conditions of various objects is wisdom waking itself up via the conditions of sights and sounds. The not finding of anything to be seen by looking nakedly at what arises is the activity of wisdom recognizing itself.[14]

5) The three preliminary parts are accumulation of merit. The fourth part, the main part, is the accumulation of wisdom. Thus the first four parts embody the two accumulations that give rise to the two fruitions in which one has become cleared out and fully

---

[14] Generally speaking, mind can be either still or moving. The first introduction deals with the mind that is being still and the second deals with the mind that is moving. By entering a shamatha that is inclusive of sinking, agitation, and rational mind's doings in general, you become involved with an approach that removes obstacles to wisdom which naturally comes forth when sights, sounds, and all the other objects of the rest of the senses appear. Overall, that puts you in a kind of one-pointedness that fits with the Mahamudra style of practice. Then, within that state, discursive thoughts might move. If they do, you look at them, and finding nothing to be seen, the thoughts, which are products of sensory appearances, turn into wisdom.

developed, buddhahood[15]. A dedication is done according to that
way in which buddhahood arises[16], saying this three times:

> By these roots of merit of mine,
> May buddhahood be accomplished for the sake of
>   migrators.[17]

That completes the verbal instructions of the Precious One, the
Jetsun from Dvagpo.[18]

*The above comes from the One Hundred Foremost Instructions, drawn
from the Collection of Written Talks given by the Lotsawa from Throphu,
Nub Jampa'i Pal.*

---

[15] Here he is making a play on the Tibetan way of writing the word for
buddha "sangs rgyas" which consists of two parts. The first, "sangs"
meaning "having been cleared out", refers to the removal of all
adventitious stains of mind, which is the fruition of dharmakaya. The
second, "rgyas" "fully developed", refers to the fruition of the form
kayas that result from having fully developed the good qualities of
enlightenment.

[16] Each type of accumulation has to be dedicated according to its own
way of being produced, which is that merit is dedicated within a
conceptual framework and wisdom is dedicated within a non-conceptual framework. The next text and its commentary say more about
this.

[17] Tib. 'gro ba. For "migrator", see the glossary. The point of saying
migrator rather than "being" or some other term is to emphasize the
wretched state of beings who are constantly forced to go here and
there from one rebirth to another by the power of their karma and so
to arouse compassion for them.

[18] "The Jetsun from Dvagpo" is Gampopa. Jetsun means a well-tamed
and person worthy of veneration. "Dvag po" is where Gampopa lived.

The Teaching:
The Instructions of Phagmo Drupa
as Transmitted by the
Drigung Founder Jigten Sumgon
by Zhamar Konchog Yanlag

Jigten Sumgon

The Source of the Jewels of Experience and Realisation,
The Ocean-Like Instructions on the Five Parts
by Zhamar Konchog Yanlag[19]

At the feet of the precious guru, the essence of every one of the buddhas of the three times, I respectfully prostrate and take refuge; grant your blessings!

Now, for what is known as the "Five-Part Mahamudra". The Protector of Migrators, Phagmo Drupa, summed up the meanings of the three baskets[20] and the four tantra sections into five systems of practice then taught them to a five-thousand strong assembly of the

---

[19] The name has some poetry included. In the Indian literary tradition and the Tibetan literary tradition copying it, the ocean is regarded as the source of jewels because it is the dwelling place of the nagas who hoard jewels. These ocean-like instructions are a source of the jewels of experience and realization. Experience means the experiences of the path which come from practice but are temporary in nature. As the path is practised, experience increases and eventually becomes realization which is final and does not change.

[20] The three baskets of the sutra teachings of the Buddha.

sangha of perfection[21]. Based on that instruction and for others who had not found certainty in the profound meaning, the founder of the Drigung Kagyu lineage who became known as Jigten Sumgon or "Protector of the Three Worlds" understood the meaning of the instructions just like an empty vessel being filled,[22] then practised them. By doing so, he accomplished the key points for each of the five parts, pacified the relevant obstacles both temporary and ultimate, and obtained, in full, every one of the ordinary and supreme good qualities. Thus he came to full knowledge of each part. He then showed that all the profound and vast instructions are for the purpose of showing the meaning he had realized and also showed that the main points of the five-part instructions are contained in what he called the "Ten Dharmas, Three Dharmas", which is a great treasury of the speech of the guru, lord of dharma, concerning the five parts.[23]

Concerning this, the precious guru said,

> First, meditate on enlightenment mind;
> Then meditate on the yidam deity;
> Then meditate on the holy guru;

------

[21] "Assembly of the sangha of perfection" means an assembly of the Vajra Vehicle sangha.

[22] This phrase is used to indicate that a disciple has attained the entire understanding of his guru.

[23] This explains how Jigten Sumgon laid out the text. He showed each of the five parts, one by one. His explanation overall includes all the instructions of the Great Vehicle—that is, contains all the key points of both paramita and vajra vehicles. In addition he added a teaching called the Ten Dharmas, Three Dharmas to the basic five-part instructions. He did this by adding a summation containing the relevant portion of the Ten Dharmas, Three dharmas, teaching at the end of each of the five parts. These two aspects can be seen further on in this text. "The guru, Lord of Dharma" refers to Phagmo Drupa.

Then meditate on Mahamudra;
At the end, seal it with dedications.

In that way, he spoke of five things. Of them, the first and last belong to the ordinary vehicle, so the middle three are the practice of the extraordinary secret mantra.

Part One: The Arousal of the Enlightenment Mind

The text called *The Rites of Meditating on the Five-Part Group* which comes from the words spoken by the Lord of Conquerors, Mikyo Dorje[24] says,

> The body is positioned in the seven points of Vairochana.
> The gentle air is held and inserted.[25]

Following on from those words, for the meditation on the three things of loving kindness, compassion, and enlightenment mind, think as follows. "Throughout my lives without beginning and for an inconceivable number of times, every one of the sentient beings has been mother to me and helped me; they have been very kind. These very kind mothers should have their kindness returned. They should be helped. They should be brought to happiness." Making the mind certain of that is loving kindness.

------

[24] Karmapa Mikyo Dorje

[25] The first line instructs the practitioner which meditation posture to assume for the practice. The second line instructs the practitioner to develop enlightenment mind through the uncommon yogic practices of wind and channels. The Five-Part system does not use these esoteric instructions but transmits the exoteric instructions which immediately follow. The author uses this quote, even though it might not seem fitting, because he is giving his readers, assumed to be Kagyu practitioners, a hint about inner possibilities.

Think as follows: "When I look at these motherly beings to see whether they have happiness or not right now, I discover that they do not. They live with the causes of unsatisfactoriness, are experiencing the results of that, and do not have the conditions for happiness. These beings ignorant of the authentic are like a blind man separated from a guide; how I feel for them. How I have compassion for each of them!" Meditating that way until you cannot bear it is compassion.

In order to free these motherly beings from unsatisfactoriness and set them in happiness, the mind that wants to attain buddhahood dons the great armour then truly and properly takes up the vows of the bodhisatva[26]. It does not entertain thoughts of its own peace and happiness even for a moment. Every thought is concerned with the welfare of others.

For this enlightenment mind, you train in fictional type of enlightenment mind in the illusion-like mode and in the superfactual type of enlightenment mind by meditating that you, and sentient beings, and unsatisfactoriness, and purposeful activity, and so on do not exist as autonomous things but are, from the outset, free of threefold production, cessation, and abiding. Engage in meditation on that for three sessions or more, until a deep-seated certainty is produced.[27]

---

[26] This is the correct spelling. All texts of the Tibetan tradition use this spelling including all the texts of the sutras and tantras that were translated in the ninth century by the greatest of Tibetan translators working with the best of Indian masters. There is a difference in meaning between the Sanskrit "satva" and "sattva", the former meaning an heroic being and the latter simply meaning a sentient being.

[27] "Fictional" and "superfactual" are better translations of a key pair of Buddhist terms that have usually been translated as "relative" and "absolute" respectively. See the glossary for more. The texts of
(continued ...)

[28] Arousing enlightenment mind like that gets to the point concerning anger, will pacify the negative forces of rgyal 'gong,[29] will bring angry states under control, will fulfill the sake of others, and causes mirror-like wisdom to dawn. Therefore, it is important to work assiduously at it; he said:

> If on the steed of loving kindness and compassion
> Others' benefit does not cut the central thread,
> In the marketplace, the kind one of men and gods will
> not arise,
> So you must work assiduously at this enlightenment
> mind.[30]

---

[27] (... continued)
Prajñaparamita, which is where enlightenment mind is explained by the Buddha, say that the training in fictional enlightenment mind is done in the manner of seeing all things as the illusions of a conjurer. In ancient India, a conjurer could conjure up illusions that appeared completely real to the audience. For instance a house could be made to appear that was fully functional. This is what is meant when talking about sensory appearances as being like illusions.

[28] Each of the five sections ends first with a statement like this about the how the particular practice gets to the points of the practice and then with a quoted verse. The statement is the relevant part of Jigten Sumgon's additional Ten Dharmas, Three dharmas material and the verse quotes what Jigten Sumgon heard from Phagmo Drupa when he heard the instructions on the Five Parts.

[29] Tib. rgyal 'gong. A type of male, negative force always connected with anger.

[30] The central thread is our normal, selfish mind, which is the backbone of an ordinary person's being. If you cut this thread using love and compassion, then you will become famous amongst all the rest of the people, gods and men, for your kindness. If you do not, then you remain an ordinary person who is nothing special.

Part Two: Creation Stage,
Meditation on the Yidam Deity

Body, skandhas, dhatus, ayatanas all are the mandala of the deity; the container world is the immeasurable mansion; the contained sentient beings are the devas and devis; and all of them have been present primordially as unification. You recognize that to be so. Now, having done so, certainty of it has to be generated and finalized.

Utter the SVABHAVA mantra, then meditate on all phenomena as empty. Within that state, from PAM comes a multi-coloured lotus, from RAM a sun disk, and on top of it from HŪM comes a crossed vajra with a HŪM letter seated on the centre of a sun disk. The HŪM's light rays become a ground, tent, and canopy of vajras outside of which a mass of fire blazes. In the centre of that pervasive protection circle that has just been made, that seed-syllable turns into a five-pointed vajra marked at the navel with a HŪM from which light radiates. The light performs the two purposes then is gathered back after which I appear as co-emergent Chakrasamvara with one face, three eyes, fangs slightly clenched, and, with bent eyebrows, a wrathful grimace. His body, dark-blue like the colour of sapphire, blazes with light. His long hair is bound up into a top-knot and at its tip is a wish-fulfilling jewel and crossed vajra. The left side is adorned with a crescent moon. He has a crown of five dry skulls and a long necklace of fifty fresh ones hanging down. The right hand of his two hands holds a nine-pointed vajra and the left inside that holds a bell, both of which embrace his consort. He has a tiger-skin skirt. He is ornamented with the five bone ornaments and the ash—the six symbols. His right leg extended stands between the breasts of red Kalaratri who is lying on her back with hands in añjali. The left leg bent presses down on and squeezes the head of black Bhairava who has his hands in añjali. In his lap is the consort Vajravarahi, red, with one face, two arms, and three eyes. Her hair is loosed and dry skulls form a crown and a long necklace. Her right hand brandishes a hooked knife. Her left hand holding a skull-cup of blood embraces the male consort around his neck. She is adorned with the five symbolic ornaments. Her two shanks are over the bhagavat's thighs; entwining him[31].

The male is marked in the three places with the three letters. The bhagavat's heart centre is marked with a white OM HA, his head with a yellow NAMA HI, his crown with a red SVA HAM HŪM, his two shoulders with black VAUṢHAṬ HE, his two eyes with orange HŪM HŪM HOH, and all the limbs with a green PHAṬ HAM; these are the six armours[32] of the hero. The female consort's navel is marked with a red OM VAM, her heart centre with a blue HAM YOM, her mouth with a white HRĪM MAM, her head with a yellow HRĪM HRĪM, her crown with a green HŪM HŪM, and between her brows with a smoke-coloured PHAṬ PHAṬ; these are the six armours of the heroine.

Light from the seed-syllable at the heart centre of the male invites sixteen jñanasatvas like the deity being meditated on and heros and yoginis surround them. The sixteen female vidyas make the offerings with argham up to shabda. By saying JAH HŪM BAM HOH the samayas and jñanas are made inseparable. Once again light from the seed-syllable at the heart centre invites the wisdom beings like the one being meditated on and these heros and yoginis make offerings.

Supplicate with OM SARVA TATHĀGATA ABHIṢHIÑCHA MAM, whereupon devis holding jewelled vases perform empowerment

---

[31] This is the special instruction from the Hearing Lineage, not the normal, outer instruction.

[32] "Armours" is shorthand for armour deities.

resultinh in the bhagavat being crowned over his head with Aksho-
bya and Vajravarahi with Vairochana.

Thinking that is the complete clarity of the visualization. Firmly
establish the pride of certainty that body, speech, and mind are the
heruka's body, speech, and mind. Recall the purities: that because
of the union of emptiness and compassion, they appear as male and
female in consort, and so on.

If you become weary of the meditation, produce a mantra garland
from the HŪṂ at the heart centre. Visualize that it goes from your
mouth into the mouth of the female consort and, cycling through
the secret places, dissolves into the seed-syllable. Saying OṂ HRĪḤ
HA HA HUṂ HŪṂ PHAṬ recite whatever is needed of the close-to-
heart, heart,[33] and so on.

When it is time to close the session, the protective circle is gathered
into the female consort, the female into the male, and the male into
the HŪṂ at his heart centre. That absorbs by steps into the flame
of the nada. Then rest in non-reference.

In that way, both the grasped-at containers and contents[34], the
ordinary appearances which entail the grasper of one's own mindstream and the grasped-at magnificent deity of the creation stage
are abandoned. Thus a form of unification that appears yet has no
self-nature, that is like a moon in water, is ascertained and that is
the finalization of creation stage.

---

[33] These are two of the various mantras of Chakrasamvara.

[34] The container worlds and the sentient beings contained within
them.

Meditating on creation stage like that gets to the point concerning desire, will pacify the negative forces of senmo,[35] will bring desire under control, will overpower appearances, and will cause individually discriminating wisdom to dawn. In brief, it is important to work assiduously at creation stage; he said:

> One's own body is the king of deity forms,
> But if not taken to the firm stage of changeless
> foundation,
> The dakinis will not assemble into a retinue around it,
> So you must work assiduously at this body, the yidam
> deity.

Part Three: Guru Yoga

The guru is a being inseparable from the wisdom present in every one of the buddhas so one takes the attitude of certainty that he is the embodiment of the three kayas and five wisdoms of a buddha whose inexhaustible sphere of ornamentation of enlightened body, speech, and mind performs the ripening and liberating of every sentient being until samsara ends. And, you take the attitude that your own mindness is inseparable from the guru because of which all the dharmas of samsara and nirvana are the nature of appearance and emptiness[36]. This attitude is called "dharmakaya devotion".

For the purpose of making a visualization of the guru, do this. Above the crown of yourself clearly seen as the deity, in space, on a lion throne, on a seat of lotus and moon, the root guru appears in the form which is the embodiment of the Jewels, the summation of the families, Vajradhara. He has a blue body, one face, and two

---

[35] Tib. bsen mo. Senmo is a type of female, negative force always connected with desire.

[36] This is a second kind of devotion, the one that results in direct perception of the dharmakaya for the practitioner.

arms, and holds a vajra and bell crossed at his heart. He is adorned with various jewelled ornaments and wears the silken pants. His feet are crossed in vajrasana. He has a peaceful mood and is surrounded by the lineage gurus, the deity assemblies of the yidam mandalas, and the dharmapalas and guards.

Giving your attention to that, worship with the seven branches—extensively or abridged, whatever—and at that time offer a mandala, including your body and your possessions in their entirety. Then, supplicate: "Glorious guru great Vajradhara, please bless my body, speech, and mind, all three."

Because of that, white, red, and blue light spring one after another from the crown, throat, and heart-centre of Vajradhara. In sequence, they dissolve into your own three places, purifying the obscurations of the three doors. Meditate on the thought that you have been made into a fortunate one whose ordinary body, speech, and mind have been manifested as the vajras of enlightened body, speech, and mind. At the close of the session, the retinue dissolves into guru Vajradhara. Then he dissolves into you and your ordinary person now becomes the guru's enlightened body, speech, and mind inseparable with your own body, speech, and mind.

Meditating on guru-yoga like that gets to the point concerning pride, will pacify the negative force of devaputra,[37] will bring prideful states under control, will give you the ability to bless others, and will cause the wisdom of equality to dawn. In brief, it is important to work assiduously at guru-yoga; he said:

> If the sun of devotion does not shine
> On the snow mountain of the guru's four kayas,
> The stream of blessings will not descend,
> So work assiduously at devotion.

---

[37] Devaputra is one of the four maras. It is the personification of evil forces which cause attraction to sense objects.

Part Four: Mahamudra

The way that mindness is present within you is not known by the rational mind of samsara and nirvana. It is not known through the exaggerations of appearance and emptiness[38]. It is not the experience of appearance. It is not the experience of emptiness. It is not the experience of existence. It is not the experience of non-existence. It is not the experience of confusion[39]. It is not the experience of liberation. It is beyond every one of those biassed positions, all of which are falls to one side or another. It is not made by a buddha. It is not created by sentient beings. It is not purified by the path. It is not a change of colour. It is primordially free from extremes. It is the fruition, the three kayas, inherent within you. It is the perfection of abandonment and realization[40]. It is the immediate brilliance having the two knowledges[41]. It is the mind that primordially is spontaneously present.

---

[38] For rational mind, see the glossary. It is a mind that deals in dualities. It is usually a samsaric mind, though there is an enlightened form of it. The exaggerations of appearance and emptiness are the concepts of appearance and emptiness produced by the rational mind. They are exaggerations because they add something to what is actually there.

[39] Tib. 'khrul pa. This term specifically means the confusion of taking what is not as what is. It is the confusion of believing that one's deluded, dualistic experiences are true, when they are not.

[40] "Abandonment and realization" is a summary of what a buddha is: all that had to be abandoned has been abandoned and all that had to be realized has been realized.

[41] Tib. mkhyen pa gnyis. The two all-knowing knowledges of a buddha: the knowledge of things as they are, and things in their extent. "Immediate brilliance" means the knowing mind that has no obscurations so is utterly bright, like the sun, and which knows not in a linear process as happens with samsaric mind, but just immediately knows whatever is.

This actuality that is the way that your innate disposition is present is called "Ground Mahamudra"[42]. It is introduced to you by means of the blessings of the guru and the method of time, then you stay in the actuality just introduced, and then you recognize that actuality is like that[43]. Just by placing yourself right on that and not fabricating anything, then staying in what that is without taints of rational mind, the essence[44] is allowed to go its own way in which concepts stop and end of themselves and then it is nakedly known as illumination[45] that is empty. This awareness, which is not a concept of illumination that has been freed of good, bad, and indeterminate concepts, does not do any recital at all[46]. This

---

[42] Tib. gnas lugs. See the glossary. This term is often translated as "natural state" which is far removed from what it actually means. The term simply means how something actually sits, how it actually is as opposed to other mistaken possibilities.

[43] Tib. dus thabs. "Method of time" is a specific style of introducing actuality. It does not mean "timely method" as is often translated.

[44] The essence of every being is "tathagatagarbha" in the sutras and "mindness" or "nature of mind" or "essence of mind" in the tantras.

[45] Skt. vara, Tib. gsal ba. The Sanskrit term and its Tibetan equivalent which are translated in this book as "illumination" are simply abbreviations of the longer terms Sanskrit "prabhasvara" and Tibetan 'od gsal, meaning "luminosity". The abbreviation in every case carries exactly the same meaning as the full word and does not represent another meaning or nuance. This is an important point because the idea has developed that there are two similar but slightly different things in the essence of mind, one called "illumination" (sometimes translated as clarity) and one called "luminosity". In fact, luminosity and its abbreviation illumination mean exactly the same. They are simply metaphors for the most fundamental quality of knowing.

[46] That is, there will none of the dualistic process whereby mind conducts its own recital, using the voice of concepts and the names that go with it, saying, "This is this, this is that, this is what is happen-

(continued ...)

staying in a state freed of names and their references is mindness, the functioning of mahamudra[47]. When you have reached the point that, no matter what conditions occur, you never pass out of that state into dwelling in one of the extremes of peace or existence, then that is called "Fruition Mahamudra".[48]

In short, if the guru does not teach it, the student will not understand it. It is the great fact beyond rational mind, the fact that cannot be experienced by rational means, that which is free from every "it is this", "it is that" made by rational mind. It is the common awareness not constructed by anyone, the state of the innate, natural condition, and that is called "Mahamudra".[49]

---

[46] (... continued)
ing", and so on.

[47] That is, the mindness experienced by the practitioner is the actual functioning of Mahamudra on the path. In other words, it is path Mahamudra.

[48] This paragraph has presented ground, path, and fruition Mahamudra in that sequence. It defines ground Mahamudra, which is the basis upon which an introduction to the nature of your own mind is made. It then states how the introduction is done and how you recognize and thus gain certainty over what has been introduced. Then, nurturing the state that has been recognized, you enter path Mahamudra in which the functioning of mindness is known. When that has been brought to finality, there is only Mahamudra, which is fruition Mahamudra.

[49] Tib. tha mal gyi shes pa. This is often translated as "ordinary mind" but that is not the meaning. Padma Karpo clearly explains that "tha mal" does not mean ordinary in the sense of common, nothing special, but means common to all, that everyone has it. It is another path term for the nature of mind.

The way of meditating on it has two parts[50]: calm-abiding and insight.

1. Calm Abiding

There are three parts to this: holding in which there is no holding; steadying of that holding; and ways of improving the steadiness.

1) The legs are crossed up. With the hands in the equipoise mudra, the shoulders are opened, the spine is straightened, the chin is hooked in a little, the lips and teeth are left to sit in their own way, and the gaze is directed down the tip of the nose, directly ahead into space. Having done that, the mind is left in its natural condition. If the mind will not abide when that is done, follow what was explained in the *King of Samadhis Sutra*:

> His body like the colour of gold,
> The protector of the world, more beautiful than all—
> Whatever mental placement is done with that as the
>   support
> The bodhisatva calls "equipoise".

For that, visualize in front of you, on a lion throne, on a seat of lotus and moon, the truly complete Buddha's[51] form and, setting the mind one-pointedly on it, do not be distracted from that object of visualization to something else. When doing that, if sinking and dullness[52] occurs, move your mental focus to the topknot, and if

---

[50] The Sanskrit terms for the two parts are shamatha and vipashyana and the Tibetan terms are gzhi gnas and lhag mthong.

[51] Skt. samyaksambuddha. This means a buddha who is a truly complete buddha as opposed to an arhat type of buddha, who is not a truly complete buddha.

[52] This is a pair of terms which are related but each of which has its own meaning. They are the two enemies of concentration on the side

(continued ...)

agitation and excitement[53] occurs, move your mental focus to your seat. You could also move the gaze up or down respectively in conjunction with that. If you follow those instructions, the problem will clear. Should there be great distraction of mind, then focus the mind on the in and out movement of breath and just by that the stream of abiding will become lengthened and eventually the abiding aspect will become steady.

2) Once abiding has been produced, visualize a white lotus at the heart centre and a drop produced from it which exits from the crown point and is ejected into space. Similarly, there is a black lotus that is facing downward and from the centre of it a black drop is produced that exits from the urethra and sits on the boundary of the seat. The mind should be held on each as they are emitted. For the former, the gaze should be raised and, when a lot of dead winds have been extracted and removed, the awareness will have been invigorated and you should rest in that. For the latter, the gaze should be lowered and, when you have worked persistently at the object of visualization, the mind can be settled and the awareness will be as before.

3) Whatever discursive thought comes up in mind because of some object—sight, sound, smell, taste, or touch—there is, so as to prevent it from continuing on to a second thought, the instruction to place mind right on the thought. Doing so brings enhancement of the equipoise. In the beginning, mind's habit of wandering away from its object will mean that many thoughts are being produced

---

[52] (... continued)
of mind being under-active. Sinking means becoming drowsy and could end in falling asleep. Dullness is the darkening of mind that happens with sinking.

[53] This is a second pair of terms which are related but each of which has its own meaning. They are the two enemies of concentration which are on the side of mind being over-active.

and capturing it again with mindfulness and alertness[54] will be difficult, however, despite the difficulty, you shouldn't be lazy. When, you have reduced the intensity of the wandering, gross discursive thoughts will have been calmed and the movement of subtle ones will be noticed. In the end, the wandering will be such that discursive thoughts will not be able to stir up the mind at all and there will be a shamatha or calm-abiding in which the actual abiding and a subsequent moment have become the same kind of thing. In that way, a calm-abiding will gradually happen.[55]

2. Insight; the Introduction[56]

When you are abiding one-pointedly in a concentrated state, investigate to see just exactly how is it with this mind that is abiding. What kind of colour does it have while abiding? What kind of shape does it have while abiding? The thought, "Well, if I don't see how it is when abiding, then I should look at it when it is proliferating" itself is a proliferation too; therefore, investigate what kind of colour it has while proliferating. What kind of shape does it have while proliferating? What kind of essence does the proliferation have? Is it visual form, sound, smell, taste, touch? How is it with this sort of thing, the opposite of abiding?

---

[54] These are the two factors of mind needed for the development of any state of concentration. See the glossary.

[55] The actual abiding and a subsequent moment which is heading towards being a discursive thought will have become the same sort of thing and, with that, the abiding does not get lost. Rather, the discursive thought gets captured by the abiding as it was starting to pop up, hence the moment following the abiding also becomes a moment of abiding, rather than a moment of distraction into discursive thought.

[56] When a person is introduced to the actuality of mind, if the introduction works, then insight or vipashyana automatically occurs.

If you do not discover mind with that, then do the following investigation. Where does it arise to begin with? Where does it stay in the interim? Where does it go at the end? You should make a thorough search for it in relation to all of these possibilities.

If you have difficulty seeing anything, offer a mandala to the guru and supplicate. Think strongly, "If I do not recognize the essence of mind, I will not be liberated from existence. If I am not liberated from that, the unsatisfactoriness of birth, old age, sickness, and death will be unbearable. Therefore, I will work only at gaining certainty in the recognition of mind". At all times exert yourself only at staring directly, nakedly at your own mind; if you do, then you will definitely see it, whatever it is.

There is no introduction without your own mind seeing your own mind; for example, if you don't see letters how will you be instructed in letters? If you see just a portion of it, then you have just that much of an introduction to it. Having looked at it, if you think it didn't appear to you, then please look at the looker itself. Not seeing it does not make it non-existent, as with treasure hidden below the ground.

Therefore, not seeing it anywhere is the supreme seeing. Henceforth, now that you understand lack of knowing as knowing, lack of consciousness as consciousness, lack of minding as minding, lack of mentation as mentation, lack of comprehending as comprehending, you will understand that as complete distraction!

Son of the family, your mind, like the horn of a rabbit, has no basis, has no nature, has no occurrence, has no arising, has no staying, has no disappearance. One's own nature being uncompounded, it is not seen even by the All-Knowing One, the Buddha. This certain fact sits nicely in your heart, therefore please rest in the state of this lack of mind itself. Please rest in the state of lack of minding. Again, son of the family, whether yours is a female mind or a male one, it is just knowing, vividly apparent and comprehending various things;

isn't this amazing? Therefore, no matter how things appear to you, rest in just this itself as it is. Rest in it relaxed. Rest in it nakedly.

Son of the family, if you hold to the idea that there is something wrong with appearance and something good about emptiness or something wrong with emptiness and something good about appearance, that is childish—appearance itself is empty, emptiness itself is apparent, so you must see appearance-emptiness as one taste!

In short, you should stay in the vast vacancy that comes with not grasping at whatever dawns and frolic in the unreality of whatever appears. Everything collapses in liberation. All is agreeable in the non-duality of samsara and nirvana. Everything is misty in the uncertainty of rigpa. All is vivid while coming and going without trace. All is brilliant in the non-duality of confusion and liberation. Please nurture the time that you can stay in this, the absence of grasping at realism.[57]

This kind of essence of mind is called "uncontrived common awareness", "the essence innate to your own mind", "the actuality that is the innate disposition of phenomena", "the way that super-fact, the dharmakaya, sits".

Isn't your mind just now present there as something cleared out, wide-awake, and brilliant? Just that is called "the self-arising rigpa essence". Don't you have the confidence that "it is just like that"? That is called "wisdom that realizes insight". In that state, isn't there something that is unquestionably present? That is called "the door of appearance of calm-abiding samadhi".

Thus, this very samsara is brilliantly evident as nirvana. These sentient beings move about as buddhas. This very confusion falls

---

[57] "Vast vacancy" is an experiential term for emptiness.

to pieces in self-liberation. Affliction itself is right there as wisdom. This, which has been understood with the name "introduction to the innate dharmakaya" or "the innate dharmakaya communicated" or "finding certainty in the innate dharmakaya" or "mastery of the dharmadhatu expanse" or "the definitive meaning of the authentic", should be kept in your heart always. And please, for this that needs no habituation, habituate yourself to it. For this fact that does not need to be preserved, please always preserve it. On account of it, abandon attachment to this life, keep impermanence in mind, always generate a mind of disenchantment, supplicate the lord, take whatever he says as a command and do it, continually wander in mountain places, goad yourself on with perseverance, look at the innate itself, and keep the introduction in your heart!

An introduction is given to disciples with those or other words that suit the level of each one's mind.

Meditating on Mahamudra like that gets to the point concerning ignorance, will pacify the negative forces of nagas, will bring delusion under control, will liberate from samsara, and causes the wisdom of dharmadhatu to dawn. Therefore, it is important to work at it assiduously; he said:

> In the vast open space of mindness,
> If there is no assurance in regard to the assembled clouds
>   of discursive thought,
> The planets and stars of the two knowledges of a buddha
>   will not twinkle,
> So work assiduously at this non-conceptual mind.

Part Five: Dedication

What is to be dedicated is included in merit and wisdom. Dedication is done on account of non-abiding nirvana, for the purposes of sentient beings. The way of making such dedication is that the dedication is done via prajña that sees the emptiness of what is to be dedicated, the dedication, and the dedicator.

Dedication like that gets to the point concerning jealousy, will pacify the negative forces of naga tsan,[58] will bring jealous states under control, will prevent loss of roots of merit, and will cause all-accomplishing wisdom to dawn. Therefore, it is important to work assiduously at that; he said:

> If the wish-fulfilling jewel of the two accumulations,
> Is not polished with prayers of aspiration,
> The fruit of your wishes will not appear
> So work assiduously at a concluding dedication.

❀   ❀   ❀

When these things have been finalized, all five topics become Mahamudra. They become: non-referencing enlightenment mind; the deity's body of inseparable appearance-emptiness; the play of the guru, samsara and nirvana; the great mudra of inseparable rigpa-emptiness; and the dedication of the encompassing purity of the three-fold sphere; and so on. And these are respectively called enlightenment-mind Mahamudra, deity's body Mahamudra, devotion Mahamudra, actuality Mahamudra, dedication Mahamudra, and so on. And, in terms of what that is equivalent to, they are universally known as "Five-Part Mahamudra". And also, viewed as preparation, main part, and conclusion, they can be taken as the practice to be done in one session and on one seat.

❀   ❀   ❀

---

[58] Tib. klu btsan. A naga-type troublesome spirit connected with jealousy and hoarding.

Urged for a long time by the great Śhākya Elder Yungja Drelwa Rinchen Gon, the one called "Subject of the Jewels" put together this expression of just the important parts of the words of the Protector of Beings, Phagmo Drupa, the words of the Protector of the Three Worlds, Drigungpa, the writings of Glorious Khachopa "Introduction to One's Own Mind", and Chokyi Drakpa Yeshe Palzangpo's "Instructions on the Five Parts". May the virtue of doing so cause all migrators to be set in meditative equilibrium on Mahamudra!

The Teaching:
The Instructions of Phagmo Drupa
as Transmitted by
All-Knowing Padma Karpo

All-knowing Padma Karpo

"Mind Harvest"
An Instruction on Five-part Mahamudra
by All-knowing Padma Karpo

Namo Mahāmudrāya

I pay homage to the fathers and sons of
Glorious Phagmo Drupa and the Siddha Ling.[59]

I bow to all those who lead migrators from the places of
    becoming,[60]
The announcers of the message of holy dharma that so
    nicely shows
Emptiness which is freedom from the four extremes of
    existence, non-existence, both, and neither
That has a core of compassion.

This, which presents nothing that has not been said
    previously
And presents just what was said previously, without
    distortion,

---

[59] The lineage of the Drukpa Kagyu starting from Phagmo Drupa,
going through Tsangpa Gyare, and then on through Lingje Repa.

[60] "Becoming" refers to sentient beings continually taking rebirth in
samsara, *becoming* one type of migrator then another, and so on.

> Was discovered through awakening that came through
>   the force of previous training's blessings and
> Given as the fruition of vast merit made previously.

The eighty-four thousand-fold dharma heap written up clearly in just a few words for the minds of those to be tamed,[61] the oral instructions that lead those who have not yet connected with the certainty of penetration[62] that comes from the vajra word empowerment[63] to the level of a buddha in one life, the special feature of the precious sugata element,[64] the instructions of the Five-Part Mahamudra, will be explained here in three parts.

---

[61] The teaching of the Buddha consists of eight-four thousand individual dharma teachings, therefore, as a whole it is called "the heap of eighty-four thousand dharmas".

[62] … of the nature of reality …

[63] The fourth empowerment of the empowerment system of the vajra vehicle is called the word empowerment. It directly introduces a person to the actuality of mind. Here, it is an elegant way of saying "introduction to the nature of mind".

[64] "Sugata element" is one of many names for sugatagarbha or buddha nature. It is the element of being that allows a person to become a sugata or buddha. When uncovered fully, it is naked reality, and that reality is called Mahamudra in this system.

I. THE EXPLANATION OF THE GOODNESS OF THE BEGINNING

A. Ordinary Procedures

1. Freedom and endowment difficult to gain

The cause is discipline, so the result, this human body, is difficult to gain. Why? Because discipline is kept to a greater or lesser extent. The essence is the eight freedoms and ten endowments. Because one is apart from the eight unfree states, there are eight freedoms. The personal and other endowments are five each making ten. A human body in general means having the support of a human body. A precious human body in particular means having the support of a human body that is rare, of greater value, of greater capability, and so on in terms of joining with dharma.

2. Impermanence

Examine your body by looking at each part from the top of the head down to the soles of the feet—which part of it is permanent? Look at the externals of place, house, and wealth and property—what do you see that is not transitory, that is truly existing there? Each passing moment brings you closer to death. There is no certainty of the time of death; as the Son of the Conquerors[65] Bhadrashri said:

> There is no assurance that you will not die even today,
> Yet you live life as though you are here for a permanent
>   stay;
> Beating your breast with your fist at the point of death is
>   not far away!

Lord Milarepa said:

---

[65] Son of the conquerors is an epithet for bodhisatvas in general.

Years and months rain down.
The droplets of fats and food strike.
This illusory house of a body is on the verge of collapse.
How ready we are for the dotted picture of death—
Ready but we have just left it too late ...

3. Karma and Its Results

Cultivating such thoughts of death again and again one then thinks
of karma and its results. Performing the ten virtues is the cause
non-ultimately of the higher levels and ultimately of buddhahood,
whereas the ten non-virtues and what goes along with them produce the three bad migrations and, even in the higher levels, only
unsatisfactoriness.

4. The Disadvantages of Samsara

No matter where you live it is unsatisfactory; no matter who you
associate with it is unsatisfactory; no matter what activity you do it
is unsatisfactory; and, moreover, it is only ever the cause of more of
the same,[66] therefore there is not one happy circumstance anywhere
in samsaric existence. The Invincible Guardian[67] said it in these
words:

---

[66] The teaching on unsatisfactoriness, the First Truth of the Noble
Ones, points out that there are two kinds of unsatisfactoriness. There
is the result, which is what we experience at any given moment, and
which we tend to think is the unsatisfactoriness being talked about in
that first truth. However, in addition to that, there is the fact that the
current unsatisfactoriness is nearly always the seed of a future result of
more unsatisfactoriness. When you realize the depth of this self-
perpetuating cycle of unsatisfactoriness, it is horrifying. And that is
the point at which renunciation comes.

[67] "The Invincible Guardian" is Maitreya, so-named because he cannot
be stopped from being the next nirmanakaya buddha in our world.

Samsara never has even
A needle-point's worth of happiness in it.
Definite happiness is nirvana alone.

B. Extraordinary Procedures

This has the three parts of: arousing the enlightenment mind; meditation on the special deity; and guru-yoga. These three being Mahamudra, they are determined to be definitive meaning. You might say, "Then it does not make sense that they should be explained as preliminaries!" However, there is no fault. These stages of the yoga to be meditated on are explained beforehand because, being associated with concept labels, they are connected with provisional meaning; if they are determined as definitive-meaning Mahamudra, they are not some meaning other than the main part to be explained. In regard to that, a person who has the preliminaries of the three refuges arouses the mind of enlightenment then works at each of all of the things to be trained in. This way of doing the meditation was what the forefather gurus accepted.

1. Arousing the enlightenment mind

You cultivate loving kindness with the thought, "If all sentient beings were to have happiness and the cause of happiness, what would be wrong with that?" In doing so, if you cannot at first produce a very vast thought, then meditate on your mother in front of you and think how it would be "If she were to obtain the happiness of nirvana ..." and "If she had the cause of happiness, that is, if she had produced the roots of merit ..." When you have trained well in that, compassion is to be cultivated: for unsatisfactoriness think, "If those inside existence were emancipated from samsara ..."; and for the causes of unsatisfactoriness think, "If they were freed from all non-virtues ..." Both of those are done first for one's mother, then for one's relatives, then for those one holds dear, and then for all sentient beings.

Compassion is explained as being of three types: in regard to sentient beings, in regard to dharma, and non-referential[68]. A three-step summary is explained as follows. *Engaging in the Middle Way* says:

> Initially, beings become attached to "I" the self and
> Produce attachment to "this" thing "of mine" and then
> Like a water-wheel pushed around, they migrate around
> Without control. Homage to compassion for them!
> Like a moon in water these pushed-around migrators
> Move around yet are seen to be empty of a nature ...

For the first one, think, "Due to permanence, singularity, and independence, these sentient beings have the unsatisfactoriness of permanence, singularity, and independence; if they were freed of karmic cause and effect ..."[69]

---

[68] The three types of compassion are explained in the following paragraphs, though the explanations depend on implication. Compassion in relation to sentient beings is compassion that sees the suffering position of sentient beings in general. Compassion in relation to dharma is compassion that arises for those beings based on understanding various aspects of profound dharma other than emptiness, for example, understanding how they are caught in the process of interdependent arising. Compassion in relation to non-referencing is compassion for sentient beings when they are seen through a mind that is not referencing them dualistically—the explanation in the text refers to it as compassion in relation to emptiness, which is saying the same thing. The first two compassions are referential, that is, they are compassion that is created in dualistic mind. The third is beyond that, it is compassion that is naturally present in non-dualistic wisdom.

[69] This is a basic teaching the Buddha gave in the first turning of the wheel of dharma. It leads a person to understand that there is no personal self in anything. It does that by pointing out that "normal" people take things to be permanent, singular, and independent,

(continued ...)

For the second one, think, "If these sentient beings having a nature of being pushed around by karma were freed from the cause and effect of unsatisfactoriness that is a reflection of being pushed around by karma, what would be wrong with that?"

For the third one, meditate on the thought, "If illusion-like sentient beings were freed from the cause and effect of illusion-like unsatisfactoriness ..." The emptiness of "move around yet are seen to be empty of a nature" is not different from being "illusion-like". In the *Vajra Essence Commentary* and others, the third step, explained as the character emptiness and its lustre compassion,[70] appears by implication under practices to be taken up.

Then there is meditation on enlightenment mind through exchange of oneself for other. Think in this way: "I give all of my happiness to others. May all others' unsatisfactoriness ripen upon me (and then think that it is purified in its own place)". And also, "May whatever pain arises in my body result in the liberation of every unsatisfactoriness of others by its ripening on me and may sentient beings have happiness".

2. Meditation on the special deity

Perform the self-visualization of yourself as your own particular deity whichever it is. Doing it so that it is fully, completely visualized is called "complete clarity". The firm attitude that the enlightened body, speech, and mind of the deity are unalterably your own body, speech, and mind is called "firm pride". Knowing that the

---

[69] (... continued)
whereas inspection shows that things are actually impermanent, composed of many parts, and arise as interdependent phenomena. Seeing the truth of this works to break down clinging to a self.

[70] Emptiness is the basic character of mindness. The lustre of that emptiness is compassion, like a polished wooden table and the shine that appears just at its surface.

shape, and so on of the body of that deity is just the play of complete purity's wisdom is what is called "the recollection of complete purity".

If the mind becomes a little weak after the yoga of that illusory body has been cultivated for a long time, turn your efforts to the recitation of the mantra as explained for the deity. When you have finished with that, the containers dissolve into the content, that into the seat, that into oneself, that into the seed-syllable mantra garland, that into the seed-syllable, and from that you enter non-referential luminosity and remain equipoised on that. Then, in post-meditation, visualisation as the illusion-like deity is done like this: whatever appears is known as the body of the deity; whatever is heard is known as its speech; and whatever thought arises is known as the play of dharmata. That has also been spoken of like this:

> If mental elaboration is made dream-like,
> Mental elaboration itself makes absence of elaboration.

3. Guru yoga

Above the crown of oneself visualised as the deity, on top of a perfect throne-seat, the root guru is clearly present as Vajradhara and atop his head the gurus of the lineage are lined up vertically in order. You create that meditation then produce the attitude that in essence they are the same in dharmata and in appearance they are a wish-fulfilling jewel that fulfills every single need and wish of those to be tamed. With that attitude, you worship with offerings of the finest things of all the animate and inanimate, and also with secret and suchness offerings. With this:

> The stage of ripened fruition of the three kayas,
> In the Dharma Palace of the place of Akanishtha ...[71]

---

[71] This is a lineage supplication prayer popular in the Drukpa Kagyu.

supplicate the line of lineage gurus from your heart, from your bones. If you want something more abbreviated, meditate on and offer to the guru himself and say this however many times:

> All mother sentient beings equivalent to space take
>   refuge in the guru, the Buddha's dharmakaya;
> Take refuge in the guru, the sambhogakaya;
> Take refuge in the guru, the compassionate nirmanakaya;
> Take refuge in the guru, the precious buddha ...

If depression and disenchantment arise and you become withdrawn and the like, if you are no longer glad at heart and your mind, turning away from the practice, no longer wants to stay on its seat, then you should visualize your guru smiling cheerily in the centre of your heart and smile, yourself, too. Whatever you see, whatever appears to you, see as the guru smiling and supplicate him or sing a nice tune, say nice words, relax your mind, be happy and open, and clear your unhappy state. If you have a lot of wild, discursive thoughts then, from within that kind of state of mixing your mind with the guru's mind, rest in an uncontrived way and supplicate and return to being un-distracted.

II. THE EXPLANATION OF THE GOODNESS OF THE MIDDLE

A. The Points of Body

The legs are crossed in vajra posture; the hands placed in the mudra of equipoise; the spine kept straight like a column of coins; the shoulders stretched out like the wings of a vulture; for the throat, the chin should be pressed in a little towards the larynx; and the eyes directed at the tip of the nose. The need for those is that they cause the winds—Downward-Clearing, Fire-Accompanying, Pervader, Upward-Moving, and Life-Holder respectively—definitely to be inserted into the central channel and then the understanding contained in the precious tantra sections is that they bring about the production of wisdom.

B. The Points of Speech

Dead winds are expelled three times then the in-breath is taken, pushed down below, and held for one period, the period for which it can be comfortably held. When it can no longer be held, it is let out, and you rest in your natural condition. Then, speech is silenced.

C. The Points of Mind

1. The method of resting the mind

Saraha said:

> Involvement with emptiness separated from compassion
> Does not get you onto the supreme path
> And meditation on compassion alone does not
> Get you to a place of emancipation in this samsara.
> Having the two joined does get you to
> Not dwelling in samsara, not dwelling in nirvana.

This means that meditation is done with prajña and method—emptiness and great compassion—unified. The actual character, emptiness, and its lustre, its shining forth as compassion, is such that when the shining forth is happening there is emptiness and, equally, when the emptiness is happening there is shining forth as compassion, so that the two are unalterably inseparable.

At this point, beginners should not think about the past, not think about the future, and not analyse the present; they should completely abandon every thought of the type "This is to be meditated on, that is not to be meditated on" and then rest in their natural condition, remaining undistractedly in that uncontrived state. Hence, the greatly accomplished one, Lord Ling said:

If you rest in the freshness of no contrivance, realisation
    will dawn;
If you preserve that like a flowing river, totality also will
    dawn.
Totally abandon all referencing with its concept labels,
Then rest perpetually in equipoise on that, Oh yogin!

In other words, having placed yourself in the way mentioned, if
thoughts proliferate and your mind will not stay still, cut them
down relentlessly and that will cause them to stop. If you nurture
resting the mind that way, it will develop greatly. That is knowing
the door of appearance of realisation through holding the mind.

The glorious Archer[72] said:

If bound, it goes off in the ten directions ...

Therefore, the way to place yourself is to let discursive thought do
whatever it wants and then to work assiduously at the mindfulness
of mere non-distraction; by doing it that way, an abiding without
proliferation of thoughts will arise. Saraha continued, saying:

If let go, it abides steadily without wandering;
I have realised that it is contrary, like a camel.

The intent here concerning the point being discussed in this
section, resting in equilibrium, is to develop the ability to stay right
on top of whatever appears and to do so without manufacturing
anything, which is then used as the place where the actual meditation is done. In other words, as was said:

This mindness which is bound in knots will be
Liberated if loosened, there is no doubt.

And, from *Hevajra*:

---

[72] "Glorious Archer" is an epithet of the Indian mahasiddha, Saraha.

If any of the unbearable karmas of beings
That are causing those beings to be fettered,
Are joined with method, then they themselves
Will release beings from the fetters of becoming.[73]

Furthermore, it also says:

Concepts themselves purify concepts and ...

If at the time of doing this meditation there is sinking, raise the
gaze to clear up the awareness. If there is agitation, relax. If there
is dullness, bring mind up again by intensifying the strength of
knowing. In that way the problems will definitely be dispelled. If
the afflictions' concepts do not shine forth as the innate purity,
work assiduously at the unification of emptiness and compassion
mentioned earlier.

2. The method of honing in on the mind

i. Honing in on the essence of mind

Investigate the essence of the mind which is resting like that—what
kind of thing is it? If you ascertain it to be luminosity-emptiness,
then examine the essence of what moves out from it, and when
something moves out from mind, look to see whether it is a two-
fold situation or not. If it is two-fold, examine how it is. If it is not
two, examine how it moves, how it stays. This so-called "luminosity-emptiness" consists of a subject of self-knowing luminosity
and an object known as empty, the two of which are not different.
Then, if you examine the essence of mind to see whether it is born
or stops, is permanent or nihilistic, comes or goes, is many or one,
you will see that it is beyond being an object of elaboration. If you
realise in direct perception what is being described, the gurus of the

---

[73] If the very thing that causes the fetters of sentient beings simply has
the right method put together with it, then the fetters themselves
become the way to release the fetters.

precious Kagyu, fathers and sons, say, "That is treading on the bodhisatva levels of the Great Vehicle".

ii. Honing in on appearance

Every appearance is one's own mind; as is said in the *Vajra Dohas*[74]:

> By that, all the dharmas, every one,
> Will be realised as one's own mind.

Generally, in relation to this appearance, on what is a single basis very many things come forth: appearances of deep delusion like a dream, an illusion, direct perception; appearances of experience. How, though, could any of them be separate from one's own mind? They could not. Therefore, when the six classes of migrators look at what we see as water in a bowl, but see different appearances, in fact those things seen are not really there as such. Similarly, one being seeing another as an enemy produces anger, one being seeing relatives produces attachment, and one being seeing others in between the two sees them with a neutral tone. All of this is one's own mind itself producing an exaggerated superfice.[75]

Regarding that, the sovereign of conquerors' sons Maitripa said:

> Phenomena, all of them, are one's own mind.
> Seen as external facts, they are the confused rational
>   mind.
> Like a dream, they are empty of entity.

He meant that sensory appearances such as the ones we are apprehending now are appearing but are empty of a self-entity. A corollary to that is that any explanation of emptiness as a non-affirming

---

[74] This is a collection of songs born of experience of the Vajra Vehicle.

[75] The superficies are the individual items experienced by the senses of a person in the fictional truth type of reality. They are exaggerations, per the earlier note.

negative is a case of being deluded over the meaning of suchness. If an objects of the senses is determined to be without truth, then grasping at truth in the appearances of the subject knowing it falls apart. The emptiness which is the hallmark of grasping at truth having been purified, the emptiness that has is explained as being established in truth, is the thought in regard to the meaning of the way things are that does not fall apart. The way of appearances is not in contradiction to the former[76]. Further to this, the Lord of Yogins, Laughing Vajra[77] said:

> From the standpoint of the superfactual truth:
> There are not, let alone blockages, even buddhas
>   themselves—

and:

> The skilful ones who realize it so
> Do not see consciousness, they see wisdom ...

Here, emptiness having the excellence of all superficies and supreme, unchanging great bliss are in unification.[78]

---

[76] This sentence reflects the Tibetan exactly. It is very terse. Padma Karpo here sums up what would take chapter of a book to explain.

[77] Milarepa made these statements in a very famous song that is studied by all Kagyu practitioners in order to understand the view correctly. The complete song together with Khenpo Tsultrim Gyatso's extensive explanation of it has been published in *The Theory and Practice Of Other Emptiness Taught Through Milarepa's Songs* by PKTC, author Tony Duff, ISBN 978-9937-572-10-1.

[78] "Emptiness having the excellence of all superficies was explained by the Buddha in the *Kalachakra Tantra*. It is not the mere vacuity of emptiness understood as a non-affirming negation, but is the vacancy of emptiness containing the fullness of all known phenomena. Supreme unchanging great bliss is the utter ease that comes with knowing the changeless situation of all phenomena, which is experienced as

(continued ...)

III. THE EXPLANATION OF THE GOODNESS OF THE END

Dedication is done by resting in the state free from referencing the three—the object of dedication, and so on. Dedication with the three is explained to be "in paramita dedication, the worldly way of dedication that references three". In that case there is: the cause of dedication, the virtue created; the object of dedication, buddhahood for the sake of sentient beings; and the words of dedication, the stainless words of the conquerors for which *A King of Aspiration Prayers, Excellent Conduct*[79], and so on should be recited. The dedications are to be done at times of arising from a session, and so on. The list of points that have been explained above in this good explanation that determines the definitive meaning is not the domain of anyone other than fortunate beings. Therefore, please make a point of keeping it very secret.

> The way of the profound and vast that has been spoken
> > of by the Capable Ones
> When realized as it is brings the unhindered definitive
> > meaning;
> I dedicate the virtue from summing that meaning up into
> > something easy to understand
> To attainment that is the finalisation of accumulating the
> > goodness of virtue.

---

[78] (... continued)
great bliss.

[79] This is a most famous prayer of aspiration by Samantabhadra, who was the Buddha's foremost heart disciple. Many Asian Buddhists recite it every day. The entire prayer with several commentaries has been published in *Samantabhadra's Prayer Volume I With Commentaries by Nagarjuna and Tony Duff* by PKTC, author Tony Duff, ISBN 978-9937-572-60-6.

Looking on from the river of a stainless intellect,
I see the horrendous conduct of those who,
Driven by karma, are wallowing in contaminated muck
And on seeing it, have a special faith in the conquerors
    and their sons.

This vast generosity of dharma give here,
Is medicine for all of those migrators;
Through it may they obtain the rank of the conquerors
And their minds be moistened with admiring faith.[80]

At the insistence of Sakyong Dondrub Dorje Palzangpo, a member of the royal caste of Sahora, the Buddhist monk Ngawang Norbu composed this in the great palace at Tagtser and had this to say:[81]

> *If you look at the glories of the higher levels, you will see that*
>   *they are the cause of unsatisfactoriness;*
> *If you look at the lower places, you will see that there is no*
>   *liberation once you are in that mire;*
> *For the classes in between, this conduct in accord with Dharma*
> *Is indeed the force that accumulates hundreds of merits!*
>
> *Involvement in worldly doings only creates more of the same*
> *And if you miss doing even one, you are harassed by all!*
> *This divine, holy dharma in which all doings are happy ones,*
> *I have, by the fortune of previous training, obtained.*

Sarva Mangalam

---

[80] Admiring faith is one of three types of faith. Admiring faith is one in which one has a very clear appreciation of the qualities of the thing and so has faith in it for that reason.

[81] It is not uncommon for a guru to make a comment to the people around him at the conclusion of some work, such as the completion of dictating of a text. These comments were sometimes preserved at the end of a text, as was done here.

The Teaching:
The Instructions of Phagmo Drupa
as Transmitted by
Situ Chokyi Jungnay

All-knowing Situ Chokyi Jungnay

A Written Instruction on Five-part Mahamudra by All-knowing Chokyi Jungnay

Nama Śhrī Gurave

The innumerable plays of becoming and peace[82]
Existing changelessly from the outset as Vajrasatva
Are the innate, the natural condition, the uncontrived guru.
I bow to that and will write a foremost instruction of
  Mahamudra.

The preliminaries of training the enlightenment mind,
Meditating on the yidam deity, and then on the guru;
The main part of staying equipoised in Mahamudra;
And the conclusion of sealing with a dedication are,
Because of being practised as a complete set in any given session,
Universally known as the "Five-Part Mahamudra".

The first of those, training the enlightenment mind, is
The fictional arousing of mind[83] which moreover is comprised of
Both aspiring and engaging types, which are like wanting to go
  and actually going.

---

[82] "Becoming and peace" means samsara and nirvana.

[83] There are two trainings in enlightenment mind corresponding to the
two levels of reality, fictional and superfactual.

55

The arousing of the aspiring enlightenment mind is as follows.
Migrators in their entirety, none of whom have not been father
    and mother,
Want happiness but, not knowing the methods of happiness,
Only engage in degrading actions, and so wander in samsara.
Understanding that, one always cultivates all-embracing loving
    kindness and compassion towards them, and
Aspires from the heart, "For their sake, I myself will accomplish
    enlightenment".
The arousing of the engaging enlightenment mind is as follows.
The causes of buddhahood are the six or ten paramitas which
Are included within the two accumulations like this:
Discipline is the accumulation of merit; prajña the accumulation
    of wisdom; and
The concentration of shamatha belongs to both.
To arouse the engaging mind is to perform them one-pointedly
With the commitment, "I will accomplish them without
    laziness".

Second is meditation on one's body as the yidam deity.
Whether you have a particular deity or not does not matter;
Meditate on the four-armed Avalokiteshvara and
Carry sights, sounds, and knowables onto the path via
Deity, mantra, and concentration, and abandon attachment to
    the ordinary.

Third, with yourself as the deity, visualise your root guru
Seated on a lotus and moon atop the crown of your head—
Great Vajradhara, the embodiment of all the Jewels,
Surrounded by the Kagyu gurus.
Now, when there is no guru, the compassionate capabilities
Of even the conquerors of the three times do not ripen the
    mindstreams of those to be tamed
And especially, the power of those conquerors hits up against
The dregs of time when beings have become totally wild.

However, the guru is able to get even these beings to produce
   just one virtuous frame of mind and,
From that start, by skilful means brings them incalculable
   benefit.
Therefore, your personal guru being equal to all the buddhas,
With an altruistic motivation, supplicate him one-pointedly.
Finally, take the empowerments of the three places, after which
The guru melts into light and sinks into you at which point
Think, "His three vajras and my three doors have become
   inseparable",
Then rest uncontrived in your natural condition.

Fourth, the main part, meditation on mahamudra, has the two
Parts of what is to be understood and what is to be practised.

For the first: the nature of the dharmas of appearance and
   becoming, samsara and nirvana,
Is the primordially-present complete purity, dharma dhatu—
Non-dual profundity and luminosity, free of extremes,
   uncompounded.
It is called "original buddha" and
"Causal mindstream" and "actuality Mahamudra" and
Is also very well known as "sugatagarbha".
In this space-like dhatu whose nature is complete purity,
Adventitious discursive thoughts stir and themselves produce
The ignorance of grasping at self and mine and the rest of the
Interdependencies in forward order, the wheel of samsara.
It, your innate disposition, is introduced to you by the guru,
Then, if the root of samsara, which is grasping at a self, and
Its root, which is discursive thought, are known, there is
A state of cessation like smoke left after extinguishing a fire.
This meditation on emptiness that has come from abandoning
Discursive thought is the supreme path of emancipation.

As for the methods of realizing it, many are taught
In Secret Mantra—creation stage, training winds, blazing and
    dripping, and so on—and innumerable ones are taught
In the sutras—shamatha's various references which are then
    determined with vipashyana, and so on—
But all of them are none other than what was just explained.
Why? Because unless emptiness is realized, it is not possible
To cross over samsara and become a buddha, therefore the
    Buddha said,
"The dharmas taught by the conqueror are for ascertaining and
    settling upon emptiness" and said
"The noble ones meditate on emptiness and that higher
    meditation
That liberates them is the fact of that".[84]

In regard to that meditation on emptiness that follows on from
    the abandonment of discursive thought:
Some Tirthikas believe it to be a "non-conceptual, supreme self"
And proceed to meditate assiduously on such a cognition; and
Some Buddhists propound it to be "the non-concept samadhi of
    Hvashang's system"
Which turns into a place where beginners' shamatha becomes
    stuck;
And, later still, there have been very famous Tibetans who for
    the most part advocated it as
A meditation which is a string of discursive thought,[85] and so on.

---

[84] In other words, the Buddha said that his teachings were given so that others could seek and arrive at the meaning of emptiness and that the higher type of meditation of his followers who had achieved the rank of a noble one, the meditation which brought about their liberation, was a meditation on the fact, as opposed to a concept of emptiness.

[85] He is referring to the Gelugpa school which is heavily criticized by the Kagyus and Nyingmas for mistaking an endless string of analytical

(continued ...)

Tainted concentrations like those are totally put aside and
Instruction is given using an experiential kind of instruction,
That is, using the foremost instructions of the lineage which are
    not mere ornaments to the word of the Conqueror,
And then the fortunate ones who have been instructed that way
Gain the experience of unifying samadhi with prajña
And this is what is accepted[86] as "path sugatagarbha" and
"Mindstream of method" and "truth of the path" and "wisdom
    accumulation".

Moreover, "samadhi" here is a shamatha one-pointedly abiding
In a non-concept type of concentration.
Such freed of concepts, unconfused luminosity-mindness
Is how all phenomena are situated and because of that
The entirety of samsara and nirvana shines forth with the deep
Certainty of realizing it as unborn and free from elaboration,
Which is explained as the meaning of "vipashyana" and "prajña".
When the practitioner is in equipoise equipped with these two,
    shamatha and vipashyana,
Because they are one entity, it is called "unification" and
For as long as equipoise and post-attainment have not become
    merged,
There is post-attainment and in it, analytical prajña is the main
    thing.

In sutra, vipashyana is termed "knowing"
And shamatha is termed its "legs".

---

[85] (... continued)
dualistic minds—which he pejoratively refers to as a string of discursive thoughts—for mind that directly sees emptiness.

[86] "Accepted" specifically means the way that the masters of the lineage
have decided upon it and proclaim it to others, they being the ones
who are in a position to make such declarations that such and such is
this way or that.

If there is no knowing by the eye,
The legs do not know the path, yet
If there are no legs, how could it be traversed?
Therefore, there is talk of "having knowing and legs".[87]

By meditating like that, the clouds in the space-like
     dharmadhatu—
Which could not have stains that are part of its nature but which
Does have the cloud-like adventitious stains of afflicted mind—
Are gradually cleared away, whereby all the classifications made
Of the ten levels and five paths; all the divisions asserted by
     Śhantipa[88]
Of One-Pointedness, Freedom from Elaboration, One Taste,
     and Non-Meditation;[89]
And so on are, together with the stains of karmic latencies,
Finally exhausted. At that point, called "complete buddhahood",
The space-pervading dharmakaya has been manifested and,
Like the light of the sun, the two fruition form kayas that
Come from merit accumulation arise effortlessly, which is
Fully known in this teaching of the Conqueror as
"The fruition mindstream" and "fruition buddha" and
"sugatagarbha possessing the two purities"[90].

---

[87] "Having knowing and legs" is a quality of a buddha.

[88] Śhantipa was one of the accomplished Buddhist masters of India. These last four are the names of the four yogas in the Mahamudra system called "The Four Yogas of Mahamudra". This system came from him to Tilopa, then Naropa, then Marpa the Translator and in that way became one of the principal teachings of Mahamudra in the Kagyu tradition.

[89] The Indian master Shantipa formulated the "Four Yogas of Maha-mudra" as a sequence of four stages of practice, whose names are mentioned here.

[90] The sugatagarbha has the original purity of being buddha-mind and
(continued ...)

Second, in the actual practice there are two methods of
   placement:
The method of placement for the body is placement with the
   seven points of Vairochana.
The method of placement for the mind is that discursive
   thoughts
Of past and future are, respectively, neither followed nor greeted
   and
The present awareness is identified using an unwavering stare
   then,
Without manufacture or alteration, one sets oneself into
   relaxation on top of that.
If thoughts are elaborated, the elaborator is identified and,
Not suppressing or furthering, not abandoning or adopting, you
   relax in that state.
If one-pointedness is not obtained, you hold the mind
By focussing on whichever support you prefer—a piece of wood
A small object, a deity's form, a seed-syllable, and so on—
And when, through gradual habituation to that, the mind has
   steadied a little,
You do short sessions many times and, at the time of the session,
At first, round up all the consciousnesses of the six-fold group
Into one via one-pointed mindfulness then
Immediately, like cutting the rope around a stook of straw,
And other than just relaxing without distraction, you abandon
Every focal point of thought concerned with the idea that this is
   the meditation to do,
Such as "is", "is not", "exists", "does not exist", "that to be
   meditated on", "this meditation",
And "bliss, illumination, and no-thought", "emptiness", and so
   on.
In the end, a mindfulness like a crow flying at its target,

---

[90] (... continued)
has the fruition purity that comes from the efforts to purify it.

A mindfulness which simply does not lose its stance,
Becomes rigpa that does what it pleases without grasping a self.
Due to that, the appearing objects of the six-fold group and
Discursive thinking about sickness and afflictions are made into
The object of the meditation then mixed with it, and that is the
     meditation.
Those things cause a non-wandering samadhi to grow.
In short, at the time of shamatha concentration meditation,
If you relax too much, the awareness will sink, and if you tighten
Too much, it will become agitated, and so it will not stay fresh.
Consideration of the faults and virtues of tightening upsets the
     mind—
It falls under the control of doubt and one-pointedness is not
     attained—
So with delight and certainty, meditate in balanced relaxation
     and tightening.
No matter which experience of bliss, illumination, or emptiness
     dawns,
If you become attached to it, you will deviate into samsara, so,
     while not clinging, and
Without suppressing or furthering, preserve an ongoing
     recognition of your self.

Then, the introduction to vipashyana is given as follows.
Guardian Maitreya said in *The Ornament of the Sutra Section*,[91]
"Understand with rational mind that there is nothing other than
     mind;
Then comprehend that that mind is empty;
Then with rational mind understand that neither exists; then
Without it, know the presence of dharmadhatu."[92]

---

[91] This text has the Sanskrit name "mahayana sutralankara".

[92] These four steps to the realization of reality through non-dual mind
are very well known. The first three are rational and hence dualistic

(continued ...)

Determine it to be so by the three of scripture, reasoning,
And valid experience as follows.
First, all appearances, the shifting events of thoughts,
Do not exist as anything other than mind alone;
For example, they should be known as the objects of a dream.
If you wonder, "How, from intangible mind, can these tangible
Things with attributes of hardness, wetness, warmth, and so on
        be produced?", then
Consider the story of the cowherd who meditated on a goat
On top of his head and ended up manifesting through mind and
        mantra a naga sprouting from the top of his head.
Given that a stable creation stage can bring the accomplishment
Even in one lifetime of the sight of the yidam deity, and so on,
Why couldn't there be the production of such things, given our
Habituation to bad karmic latencies since beginningless time?
In one cup of water, the devas see nectar,
Whereas the pretas see pus and blood, and
The beings who live in the ground see a good home
Where humans see ordinary earth and stones, and so on,
Which is a sign that such is only an appearance of mind with no
        truth to it.
When in that way you have made certain that apparent objects
Are mind, you must know that the mind also is emptiness.
Mind has not so much as an speck of existence to it.
How is that? At the time of appearances conditioned by objects
Of clinging, they are just known, just flicker on and off, just arise
        and cease by the instant.
Moreover, if the individual items of the eight-fold group of
Consciousness are, each one, cut at the base, the root is
        destroyed.
The so-called "alaya" is nothing other than a name.
For example, just as a mirage has no water in it but

---

[92] (... continued)
approaches, the last is non-dual.

Thirsty animals, confusing it for water, chase after it,
So this extreme liar of a mind that grasps to a self then
Accumulates bad karmas is more than very confused!
Therefore, the Conqueror, in the sutra section,
Clearly said, "Do not involve your mind with mind!"
If one becomes without mind, that leaves its nature,
Which he said "is luminosity" and which clung to is
So-called "mind", the eight-fold group of consciousness,
And their nature is confusion, a discursive thought.
Mind's nature called "luminosity" is
Non-thought, not-confused, self-knowing wisdom.
That is not obtained by meditation that newly creates something,
Nor is it bestowed by the compassionate activity of the
      conquerors;
Rather, the lineage of the causal mindstream has been
      beginninglessly present as your nature and
It is your accumulation of the accumulations, purification of the
      obscurations, and force of meditation
Combined with the introduction to it made by the blessings of a
      realized guru
That makes you see what you have. Therefore, it was said,
"Co-emergence, that which cannot be expressed by another,
Is not something that can be found anywhere;
Rather, it has to be known through reliance on the
Glorious guru's method of time and through one's own merit."[93]
      [94]

That kind of co-emergence, your nature freed from both
The object grasped at and the mind that is the grasper, which is
Pure like space and does not fall into sides that have been set up,

---

[93] Co-emergence is the name for reality according to the Sahajayoga
(Co-emergence Yoga) system of Mahamudra that came down through
Saraha.

[94] This is a verse from the *Hevajra Tantra* which is commonly quoted
throughout the Kagyu schools.

A unification of shamatha and vipashyana that sees freedom from
    elaboration,
"Will, if you can stay in equipoise on it for even one moment,
Defeat the darkness accumulated during a kalpa", it was said.[95]
Mahamudra with the view of freedom from elaboration like that
Is the heart of the views of both sutra and tantra.
Master Nagarjuna and others state that "there is no view higher
    than the Middle Way, Madhyamaka", but
The *Lamp of the Modes* says they are of "the same meaning"
    meaning that the views are the same in meaning.[96]

Therefore, if you have taken hundreds of unsurpassed
    yogatantra's
Four empowerments and are empowering others with them,
Given that the meaning of the fourth empowerment is
    Mahamudra
What need is there to raise the issue of your own practice of it?
If just the name is heard, the ears are covered, so what difference
Is there from the activities of the governor of the desire realm?[97]

---

[95] ... by Tailopa.

[96] Those expounding the sutras say that the Middle Way—Madhya-maka—is the highest view, but when the matter is carefully examined, that view and the view of Mahamudra are not different, as mentioned in a number of tantric texts, such as the well-known *Lamp of the Modes*.

[97] The person bestowing the empowerment, which is none other than Mahamudra, must be able, through his own practice of it, to make the actual meaning dawn in the minds of the disciples requesting the empowerment. If people hear the fancy-sounding name "Mahamudra" but do not have the experience of it dawn in their minds, then they might as well have had their ears covered. And if their ears were covered and they were did not hear the instructions that would open their minds to Mahamudra, then what difference would there be between their activity in taking the empowerment and their normal
(continued ...)

When meditating on that sort of yoga of unification,
If you start to cling to[98] bliss, illumination, and no-thought, then
You will deviate into the desire, form, and formless realms
    respectively,[99]
Hence you have to preserve it by not clinging to it and not
    stopping it but letting it be present of itself.
Furthermore, discarding all the rational-mind-made tenet
    systems which have come from the sophistry
That has the conceit of believing that just intellectual
    understanding is sufficient;
Referencing emptiness after the collapse of appearances;
Becoming afraid like when peering over the edge of a precipice,
When there is a small cessation of discursive thought;
Seeing it as faulty whenever discursive thought arises; and so
    on—
You then practise with diligence according to the system
Of the oral instructions of practice adorned with experience.
The state is preserved by allowing whatever arises to arise; by not
    constructing anything within the natural condition;
By non-distraction and non-meditation; by resting relaxed; and
    so on.
At that time, wisdom shines forth from the heart and
    exaggerations are cut.
Without your wanting them, the signs of the path and good
    qualities will increase.

---

[97] (... continued)
activities, driven by dualistic mind, given that dualistic mind is the
governor who creates and maintains this desire realm they live in?

[98] ... the experiences of ...

[99] If you cling to any of the three temporary experiences that arise
because of having meditated, that will create the cause for rebirth in,
that is, you will deviate from the true path into, one of the three realms
of samsara.

Like mercury spilled on the ground, drops of the eight
    dharmas[100]
Will not mingle with your practice; you will find all of the
Enjoyable pastimes of samsara distasteful as poison.
Understanding that emptiness and dependent relationship must
    be unified,
If method and prajña are brought together and the two purposes
    are spontaneously accomplished,
Then "virtuous practices have gotten to the point", as is said.
In that way, the three preliminaries accumulate merit and
The main part accumulates wisdom so the fruition of
The two accumulations, the two or three kayas, is gained.

Moreover, the point when the two luminosities of ground and
    path mix,
Which is known as "the meeting of mother and son",
Is called "complete buddhahood" and at that time
The essence empty, dharmakaya,
The nature luminosity, sambhogakaya, and
The liveliness appearing without stoppage, the universal
    nirmanakaya, are
Totally complete, which is the mahasukhakaya.
The primordial actuality that is the nature of the four kayas,
Is the self-recognized, supreme fruition because of which
It was said to be "the fruition divorced from hope and fear".

Fifth, for the conclusion, there is sealing with dedication.
The lines, "In the mandala of self-knowing sugatagarbha,
The virtue accumulated of the two accumulations" are saying
"All the virtue as much as there is in the three times".
Then, in the state that holds to the view of emptiness

---

[100] Mercury that has been spilled breaks into little droplets that do not
mix with anything. Let the poisonous little bits of the eight worldly
dharmas scatter and not mix in with your practice.

Which does not reference the threefold sphere of
Action, actor, and object of dedication now drawn together as
     one,
Dedicate one-pointedly so that yourself and others, all migrators,
Become quickly released from this cage of samsara,
So that they attain the rank of the Mahamudra of unified co-
     emergent wisdom.

Moreover, no matter how vast the merit that has been
     accumulated,
If the dedication is not held within the view of total purity of the
     threefold sphere, then,
As the Conqueror said in the Prajñaparamita and other sutras,
It will be like a feeble person without eyes and
Like eating food mixed with poison.
Thus, so that you do not veer away from making it into
A faultless cause of emancipation, take care at all times and,
No matter which virtuous practices of the creation and
     completion
Yogas you do, make an effort to plant seeds of enlightenment!

In that way, within one session five branches
Are practised as a set, though for beginners
When doing the main part—holding the mind, and so on—and
The meditation and familiarization is going well, it is not
Necessary to shift to from the unification yoga to another
     practice.

Then, as an adjunct to that, the practice can be connected to the
     time of day.
At dawn, there is "the yoga of making wisdom clear":
Immediately on waking, without letting discursive thoughts
Get in the way, identify the rigpa of unified luminosity-
     emptiness
And rest in equipoise on the innate character.
Meditate on strong compassion for

All of the migrators who have not realized it, then begin your
    virtuous practice.
That grooms the meditation and provides a good start.
It is the foremost instruction for getting into the system of
    virtuous practice.

When day arrives, there is the yoga of sealing appearances;
It is a foremost instruction connected with purifying the
    confusion of appearances in their entirety.

At dusk, there is the yoga of carrying desirables onto the path as
    assistants:
Not being overly attached to food, drink, clothes, bedding,
And so on, but remaining in the state that knows them as empty,
Train in them as dharmata itself sinking into itself.
If you are incapable of that level, then train in them
As possessions that are offered to the deity and guru.
It is the foremost instruction for completing the accumulations
    without being bound by desirables.

In the early night, there is the yoga of gathering the sense
    faculties into the ground:
In order to prevent whatever confused thoughts shone forth
    during the day
From continuing further, stare unwaveringly at their essence.
It is the foremost instruction of remaining within virtuous
    practice at night.

At midnight, there is the yoga of inserting consciousness into the
    vase:
Supplicate the heart mandala[101] without meditating on it;
Sever discursive thoughts and go to sleep in equipoise
On dharmata free of elaborations.

---

[101] The mandala of the heart chakra, which is the home of luminosity.

That, at this time and the time of death, is the
Oral instruction for mixing mother and son luminosities.
At the point of death, if you intend to perform the yoga of
The direct crossing into wisdom, you will sever the clinging of
     attachment to all things,
Lay aside every wrong-doing and downfall of this and all other
     lives,
Bring to mind every virtue of self and others then rejoice in
     them,
Then dedicate your merits to the great enlightenment.
Especially, if you can manage it, you should make the body into
     an offering:
Having decided that your own mind has no birth or death,
Give up on the dissolution stages and the rest, and,
Not engaging in many different visualizations
Set yourself in equipoise in the greater mudra, placing yourself in
     your natural condition
Without an atom of meditation or non-meditation,
And transfer your mind to the expanse of the dharmakaya in full
     unhindered view.
That, which closes the doors to the bad states of the
Bad migrations and eliminates the confused adoption of
Samsara in general and especially the intermediate state,
Is the foremost instruction for realizing death as the dharmakaya.

The small instruction on the Five-Part Mahamudra,
A work not so large, was composed after the
The Great Sawang of Derge's personal advisor,
Drepo Chosong Lodro, pressed for it verbally.
The author, who wrote down whatever came to mind
In an outpouring of unrestrained blather,
Is named Tsuglag Chokyi Jungnay.

PART 2

Benchen Tenga Rinpoche's
Oral Commentary to
"The Source of the Jewels of
Experience and Realization",
The Ocean-Like Instructions on The
Five Parts

The Third Benchen Tenga Rinpoche

The Enlightenment Mind
Is the Motivation For Studying the Teaching

The Buddha has said that any roots of merit, whether worldly or dharmic, done with a motivation connected with virtuous states of mind become meritorious, whereas roots of merit done with a motivation influenced by non-virtuous states of mind such as pride, jealousy, aggression, and so on are of little benefit. Therefore, it is necessary to take up a motivation of doing whatever we do for the sake of enlightenment.

As the conqueror's son, Shantideva said:

> All other virtue is like the plantain tree;
> When its fruit has been produced, it is exhausted.
> The living tree of enlightenment, even though
> Its fruit is produced, never ends but increases.

This means that whatever roots of merit are planted with a motivation that has enlightenment mind with it grow more and more until enlightenment is reached, like a living tree that only grows larger and larger and improves further and further as its fruits are produced, whereas all roots of merit planted with a motivation that does not have enlightenment mind with it produce their fruit and then, like plantain trees,[102] are finished and of no further use.

---

[102] The Plantain tree grows, produces fruit once, then dies. Karma
(continued ...)

Thus, you should now arouse this enlightenment mind and, in order to do so, should think like this, "All sentient beings equivalent to space whose nature at present is suffering, who like a blind man do not know the true path, who are only ever experiencing unsatisfactoriness, have only ever been my very kind mothers and fathers. In order to lead them to the level of a buddha, I will study the instructions of the Five-Part Mahamudra". With that kind of thought of enlightenment mind clearly in mind, say the refuge prayer three times:

> I take refuge in the Buddha, Dharma, and Supreme
>   Assembly,
> Until becoming enlightened.
> By my merit from practising giving and so on,
> May I accomplish buddhahood for the sake of all
>   migrators.

---

[102] (... continued)
made with normal, samsaric mind works in exactly the same way. However, karma made with enlightenment mind is like the usual fruit tree that produces its fruit but then lives on, producing fruit over and over again.

Homage and Preamble

The text that I will be explaining here is *"The Source of the Jewels of Experience and Realization", The Ocean-Like Instructions on The Five Parts*. The text was written by the fifth Zhamarpa of the Karma Kagyu lineage in the 1500's. Zhamar's text is a commentary on a text by the founder of the Drigung Kagyu which includes both the Five-Part instructions as given by Phagmo Drupa and what is called the "Ten Dharmas, Three Dharmas", a set of oral instructions on the Five-Part Mahamudra that came to the founder of the Drigung Kagyu when he had realized the meanings of the five parts through diligent practice of Phagmo Drupa's instructions.

What I will be doing here is giving an explanation of the fifth Zhamarpa's text which will, because of what has just been explained, include the original Five-Part instructions transmitted by Phagmo Drupa and the "Ten Dharmas, Three Dharmas" transmitted by the founder of the Drigung Kagyu. The text by the fifth Zhamarpa is contained in its entirety earlier in this book. However, to make it easier for the reader, the relevant portions of Zhamarpa's text are quoted here and marked off in italics, and commented on.

Zhamarpa's text starts out with a homage to the author's guru, seen as all the buddhas embodied in one person: *At the feet of the precious guru, the essence of every one of the buddhas of the three times, I respectfully prostrate and take refuge; grant your blessings!*

Zhamarpa's text continues by saying, *Now, for what is known as the "Five-Part Mahamudra"* ... The instructions that Zhamarpa is about to elucidate are instructions on: Mahamudra that comes from meditating on mind as enlightenment mind; Mahamudra from meditating on the body as the form of the deity in creation stage; Mahamudra from meditating on guru-yoga; Mahamudra from meditating on calm-abiding and insight; and the concluding Mahamudra of dedication. Thus it is a set of instructions of Mahamudra in five parts and so is called The Five-Part Mahamudra. It is a set of instructions which, if practised, brings experience of Mahamudra, which is the name in this system for ultimate reality.

How did this teaching come into the world? Here is a short history that shows how this profound teaching appeared in this world and was transmitted from one generation to another. First, our teacher Shakyamuni Buddha, for the sake of complete enlightenment, accumulated merit throughout countless numbers of aeons and then, having gone to the vajra seat at Bodhgaya, manifested truly complete buddhahood. Then the chief of the gods, Kaushika, requested the Buddha to turn the wheel of dharma and show the eighty-four thousand dharmas. Following his request, the Buddha turned the first wheel of the Four Truths of the Noble Ones at Varanasi, the middle wheel of No-Characteristics at Vulture Peak Mountain, and the final wheel of Fine Distinctions not at a specific place but at various places. Then, following that, at the request of various individuals, as with King Indrabodhi who requested and was taught the Guhyasamaja tantra, and the bodhisatva Vajragarbha who requested and was taught the Chakrasamvara tantra, the Buddha taught the unsurpassed secret mantra section with its four tantra sections by turning what is called "the unfathomable wheel of dharma".

Many beings practised and gained experience of those teachings of the causal characteristic and fruition vajra vehicles. Thereby, uncountable numbers of pandits and many siddhas, such as the eighty-four mahasiddhas, appeared in India. One of the eighty-four mahasiddhas was the one called Tailopa. From an ultimate perspective, he attained all the empowerments, instructions, and inner instructions directly from the dharmakaya Vajradhara; as he said himself:

> I, Tailopa, have no human gurus;
> My guru is dharmakaya Vajradhara.

From a conventional perspective he relied on gurus of four lines of transmission: Nagarjuna, Master Krishnapada, Lavapa, and Dakini Kalwa Zangmo. He requested and received from them the complete empowerments, oral transmissions, and foremost instructions of the father tantra Guhyasamaja, the mother tantra Mahamaya, the essence Hevajra, and the final ascertainer, Chakrasamvara. In addition, he obtained all the special instructions that later became known as the Six Teachings of Naropa, whose four root teachings are Fierce Heat, Illusory Body, Dreaming, and Luminosity. When those were put together with the four lines of transmission, they became called the Eight Precepts.

Then there was Tailopa's disciple the mahasiddha Naropa. Naropa attended Tailopa, went through twelve trials, and at the end realized all that Tailopa had realized about Mahamudra.

Then there was Naropa's disciple, the Tibetan man called Marpa the Translator. Naropa gave all of the empowerments and instructions to Marpa and Marpa carried their texts back to Tibet where he translated them into Tibetan. In Tibet, Marpa had many students and four main disciples. Of the four, Marpa gave all the empowerments and instructions to Milarepa. Then, Milarepa had many yogin disciples but there were two especially great sons—Lord Gampopa who was like the sun and Rechungpa who was like the moon. Gampopa received all of the instructions from Milarepa then went to Gampo Hills. It is said that he had 51,600 disciples. Of them the most important ones were a group of three men called The Three Men of Kham. They were Khampa Grey-Hair who later became known as Karmapa Dusum Khyenpa, Khampa Dorgyal who later became known as Sugata Phagmo Drupa, and

Saltong Shogom whose incarnations many lifetimes later became known as Traleg Rinpoche.

Zhamarpa's text then says, *The Protector of Beings, Phagmo Drupa, summed up the meanings of the three baskets and the four tantra sections into five systems of practice then taught them to a five-thousand strong assembly of the sangha of perfection.* When Sugata Phagmo Drupa practised his guru's instructions on Mahamudra, he practised them as a set of five instructions. At one time he taught Mahamudra to an assembly of five thousand of his students. On that occasion, he summed up all the meanings of Vinaya, Sutra, and Abhidharma—all the teachings of the eighty-four thousand dharmas—and all the meanings of secret mantra into the set of five, special, oral instructions. That was the beginning of a style of teaching Mahamudra that continued and was henceforth generally called "the five-part instructions of Mahamudra".

Zhamarpa's text continues with this. *Based on that instruction and for others who had not found certainty in the profound meaning, the founder of the Drigung Kagyu lineage who became known as Jigten Sumgon or "Protector of the Three Worlds" understood the meaning of the instructions just like an empty vessel being filled, then practised them. By doing so, he accomplished the key points for each of the five parts, pacified the relevant obstacles both temporary and ultimate, and obtained, in full, every one of the ordinary and supreme good qualities. Thus he came to full knowledge of each part. He then showed that all the profound and vast instructions are for the purpose of showing the meaning he had realized and also showed that the main points of the five-part instructions are contained in what he called the "Ten Dharmas, Three Dharmas", which is a great treasury of the speech of the guru, lord of dharma, concerning the five parts.*[103]. The founder of the Drigung Kagyu lineage, who

---

[103] This explains how Jigten Sumgon laid out the text. He showed each of the five parts, one by one. His explanation overall includes all the instructions of the Great Vehicle—that is, contains all the key points

(continued ...)

became know as "Jigten Sumgon" or "Protector of the Three Worlds", was in the assembly and received these teachings from Phagmo Drupa in their entirety. Jigten Sumgon then practised each of the five parts, realized the key points associated with each of the five parts, cleared the obstacles associated with each of the five parts, and obtained all of the ordinary and supreme accomplishments connected with each of the five parts. By doing so, he gained very special qualities.

Sugata Phagmo Drupa's actual words were recorded in writing by Jigten Sumgon and the text continues by giving the exact words of *"the precious guru"* as it says, meaning the words of Phagmo Drupa himself. Phagmo Drupa laid out the five parts with the following words:

> *First, meditate on enlightenment mind;*
> *Then meditate on the yidam deity;*
> *Then meditate on the holy guru;*
> *Then meditate on Mahamudra;*
> *At the end, seal it with dedications.*

In that way, he spoke of five things. Of them, the first and last belong to the ordinary vehicle, so the middle three are the practice of the extraordinary secret mantra. This means that, of the five special instructions in this teaching, the first and the last—meditation on enlightenment mind and sealing with dedication—are dharma instructions that belong to the common vehicle. The remaining three—body as body of the deity through creation stage, unification with the

---

(... continued)

of both paramita and vajra vehicles. In addition he added a teaching called the Ten Dharmas, Three Dharmas to the basic five-part instructions. He did this by adding a summation containing the relevant portion of the Ten Dharmas, Three dharmas, teaching at the end of each of the five parts. These two aspects can be seen further on in this text. "The guru, Lord of Dharma" refers to Phagmo Drupa.

guru, and Mahamudra meditation—are oral instructions of the uncommon secret mantra vehicle.

Jigten Sumgon combined those instructions of his guru, Phagmo Drupa, with instructions of his own that came from his specific way of practising Phagmo Drupa's instructions. The combined instructions of Phagmo Drupa and Jigten Sumgon were written down and became the text shown in italics, here. The necessary pre-amble has been given and now the text turns to the actual instructions.

In order to enter the secret mantra vehicle, it is necessary to receive an empowerment of secret mantra. The empowerment is the necessary gateway to being able to practice the teaching. The instructions on how to practise are provided after empowerment has been bestowed.[104]

---

[104] It is clearly stated in the tantras that a ripening empowerment must be given to the disciples first before the liberating instructions are bestowed and also, before they can be realized. Accordingly, if you want to do these practices and have not had a proper empowerment, you should seek a teacher, obtain an empowerment, then receive the instructions on the practice. This book can then serve as a support for your guru's instructions.

Commentary to the First of the Five Parts, Enlightenment Mind

In meditation on the enlightenment mind, the meditation has all sentient beings for its reference. The reason for this is that, generally speaking, throughout all of our successive lives without beginning, every sentient being has been at times our mother and at times our father. As the text says, *Throughout my lives without beginning and for an inconceivable number of times, every one of the sentient beings has been mother to me and helped me; they have been very kind.* When you look at it that way, you learn that all of these beings have really loved us and been exceptionally kind to us. However, these same, kind beings have developed wrong attitudes and practices for themselves; as Shantideva said:

> They want to get rid of suffering but
> End up just making more suffering.
> They want happiness but due to delusion
> Destroy their own happiness as though an enemy.

Sentient beings want to get rid of their problems but, not knowing the right way to go about it, usually end up doing bad actions that only ever cause more obscuration for them. And, sentient beings would like to have perfect happiness, however, because of their obscurations, they destroy whatever happiness they have just as though it were their enemy. These wrong attitudes and practices make them into an object of compassion.

Because of seeing their kindness and because of the compassion that comes for them given their situation, the thought comes that we should act on their behalf so as to benefit all of them. How could we do that? We are people who have obtained a precious human birth, put ourselves under the care of a guru or virtuous spiritual friend, and taken up the various spiritual practices for developing body, speech, and mind. If we were to do our practices with the thought of completely removing the unsatisfactoriness of all these sentient beings currently caught in unsatisfactoriness, then there would be a very great benefit produced for all of them. Thinking like that, that all the roots of merit we accumulate through whatever we do with body, speech, and mind and also with meditation should be done for the purpose of providing complete happiness, both temporary and ultimate, for all these sentient beings, is the very thought needed for the enlightenment mind meditation. We should think that way again and again.

The words of the text quoted just above, at the beginning of this section, are mainly concerned with developing the thought of loving kindness. After that, for the development of compassion, the text says, *Think as follows: "When I look at these motherly beings to see whether they have happiness or not right now, I discover that they do not. They live with the causes of unsatisfactoriness, are experiencing the results of that, and do not have the conditions for happiness"*. If we investigate whether sentient beings have happiness or not, we find that they do not and that they have nothing but unsatisfactoriness. If we consider the hell-beings, they only ever have the sufferings of heat or cold; if we consider the pretas, they only ever have the sufferings of hunger and thirst; if we consider the animals, they are perpetually caught in servitude. For human sentient beings, the Buddha pointed out many types of suffering: they have what he called "the four great sufferings" or "the four rivers of suffering" which are birth, aging, sickness, and death and moreover, they have what he called the eight sufferings, the three sufferings, and so on—so, even those who take a human birth have suffering. Then, the asuras, because they constantly engage in fights, have the suffering of fear.

Then, the gods, although they have a most excellent life while they are alive, have their own specific sufferings of change at the end of that life. In sum, when you examine the six classes of sentient beings, you find that there is not one who has a satisfactory situation.

You might wonder, "Well, how is it that these beings perpetually experience suffering?" It is like this. All sentient beings have delusion. On the basis of the delusion, the poisons of the five afflictions arise in mind and because of that karmas are accumulated on the mindstream. Based on those karmas, the various types of unsatisfactory existence come about. For example, because of anger and jealousy, karma is accumulated that leads to the experience of the sufferings of the hell realms; because of desire and covetousness, the sufferings of the pretas appear; because of stupidity, the sufferings of the animals appear, and so on.

You might wonder, "When did this unsatisfactoriness begin?" Lord Gampopa said, "Samsara is beginningless". There is no initial point at which it started; whatever we do, there is always unsatisfactoriness.

You might wonder, "Does unsatisfactoriness come to an end of its own accord?" The answer is no; it does not end by itself. To rid ourselves of it, you must make the effort to follow a path of dharma, of reality, so that you reach the level of a buddha. Then you will be relieved of unsatisfactoriness and will not experience it any longer.

These beings ignorant of the authentic are like a blind man separated from a guide; how I feel for them. How I have compassion for each of them!" Meditating that way until you cannot bear it is compassion. These beings are ignorant of reality, which is also called "the authentic" in Buddhist teaching. They do not know of the needs to abandon bad action, get rid of the obscurations, accumulate virtue, and correctly understand karma and its cause and effect. Sentient beings by themselves do not know of the possibility of buddhahood and cannot find their way to it without assistance. They are like blind people who have no guide and hence cannot see their destination and cannot get to it. When you see that sentient beings are like this, compassion arises for them.

At this point, you should have a stronger kind of thought that you need to liberate, to free, these very kind mother and father sentient beings from the unfathomable sufferings experienced by the six classes of migrators. Because of that, you come to the certainty that you need a method to help them attain a state of perfection. Thus, the text says, *In order to free these motherly beings from unsatisfactoriness and set them in happiness, the mind that wants to attain buddhahood dons the great armour then truly and properly takes up the vows of the bodhisatva*. In order to do what you have decided to do, first, as Nagarjuna said, you need to don the great armour of strong determination, the courageous attitude that you will go ahead no matter what it takes. It helps to meditate a little on patience at this point, thinking of the difficulties that you will have to go through while working for all sentient beings, difficulties such as being ridiculed or denigrated by others. Then, with that kind of determined courage and aware of the magnitude of the task, the next step is to commit yourself to the path of the bodhisatva by taking the bodhisatva vows. The vows can be taken in front of a virtuous spiritual friend or otherwise in front of a visualisation of all the buddhas and bodhisatvas. In the latter case, think that you undertake the same commitment as the previous buddhas and bodhisatvas did and then think that you have actually received the vows. The bodhisatva vows should be taken again and again.

The person who has entered training on the bodhisatva path maintains the enlightenment mind at all times. The mind of the bodhisatva *does not entertain thoughts of its own peace and happiness even for a moment*. On this path, never mix thoughts of doing your practice for a longer life or freedom from illness or great happiness in with your practice. *Every thought is concerned with the welfare of others*. Your mind should always be taken up with enlightenment mind. Whatever roots of merit you create should be done for the purpose of the migrators in the six realms of existence and should be done as part of furthering the enlightenment mind.

There are two types of enlightenment mind, fictional and super-factual, and each has its own, specific training. Thus the text says, *For this enlightenment mind, you train in its fictional level in the illusion-like mode and in the superfactual level by meditating that you, and sentient beings, and unsatisfactoriness, and purposeful activity, and so on do not exist as autonomous things but are, from the outset, free of the three of production, cessation, and abiding.*

For the practice of the fictional type of enlightenment mind, the thought of enlightenment mind is developed through the two thoughts of loving kindness and compassion. These correspond to the first two of the four limitless ones. In the first one, we make the prayer:

> May all sentient beings have happiness and the cause of happiness.

This is a prayer that all sentient beings will have perfect happiness, non-ultimate and ultimate. Perfect happiness comes about because of having its cause, perfect virtue, so we also pray that sentient beings will travel the path of developing perfect virtue. This wish for their happiness is the thought of loving kindness; meditate on it again and again. Then, in the second of the four immeasurable thoughts, we make the prayer:

> May all sentient beings be free from suffering and the cause of suffering.

This is a prayer that all sentient beings will be taken beyond their unsatisfactory situations. For that to happen, they need to be freed from the causes of unsatisfactoriness. The wish that they have this is the thought of compassion; meditate on it again and again![105]

For the superfactual type of enlightenment mind, the three parts of any activity done with enlightenment mind: the meditator; the object of the meditation which is all sentient beings; and the act of meditating on the thoughts that all sentient beings should be freed from suffering and its cause, and should have happiness and its cause, and so on are seen to be from the outset not existent. This is done by staying in equipoise in the state in which mind to begin with is not produced, in the interim does not abide, and in the end does not cease.

As the text says, *Engage in meditation on that for three sessions or more, until a deep-seated certainty is produced.*

At the end of the instructions for each of the five sections there is a part spoken by Jigten Sumgon himself. He adds his own special instructions to clarify the effects of practising the instructions of the section. The text says, *Arousing enlightenment mind like that gets to the point concerning anger, will pacify the negative forces of rgyal 'gong, will bring angry states under control, will fulfill the sake of others, and causes mirror-like wisdom to dawn. Therefore, it is important to work assiduously at it.* If you meditate on loving kindness and compassion like that again and again, it will reduce anger; in other words it becomes an antidote to anger. Furthermore, it causes the mind that is involved with "the sake of others"—that is, a mind that concerns itself with fulfilling others' aims, the aims of all sentient beings—to

---

[105] These are the instructions on the development of loving kindness and compassion that go with the Five-Part Mahamudra. There is a second set of instructions for developing loving kindness and compassion; it is taught in the system called Mind Training that was brought to Tibet by Atisha. In that system, loving kindness and compassion are developed using a five-fold practice which includes the meditation called "Sending and Taking".

develop and become very great within you. Furthermore, of the five wisdoms, it causes mirror-like wisdom to dawn within you because the deluded aspect of the energy called anger has been overcome and the wisdom aspect of anger thus revealed is the mirror-like wisdom.

Then, at the end of each section, there is a verse from Phagmo Drupa himself, quoted by Jigten Sumgon, summing up the need for practising the instructions of the section. Phagmo Drupa said:

If, on the steed of loving kindness and compassion,
Others' benefit does not cut the central thread,
In the marketplace, the kind one of gods and men will not
*   arise",*
So you must work assiduously at this enlightenment mind.

Here, loving kindness and compassion are likened to a steed. A very good, fast steed becomes famous. If you develop the steed of loving kindness and compassion within yourself, you could bring great benefit to all sentient beings. If you do, you will cut the central thread that is our normal, selfish mind, and which is the backbone of an ordinary person's being. Then you will become famous amongst all the rest of the people, gods and men, for your kindness; if you do not, then you will remain an ordinary person who is nothing special. If you do, they will talk about how kind you are to them and news of you will spread throughout their meeting places. In other words, you will become the talk of the town for both gods and men. Therefore, you should work assiduously at the enlightenment mind.

Commentary to the Second of the Five Parts, Creation Stage

The second of the Five Parts is the creation stage meditation of what is called a personal deity in Sanskrit language and a yidam deity in Tibetan language. Overall, the profound, secret mantra path that can lead to enlightenment in this body in one lifetime was presented by the Buddha in two, main parts called creation stage and completion stage. Creation stage is the practice of meditating on one's ordinary body as the body of the yidam deity.

The Buddha taught many different yidam deities: some appearing in the male form, others in female form; some with one face and two arms, some with one face and six arms; some wrathful and some peaceful. Nonetheless, because they are nothing other than the luminance of the dharmakaya, they are actually the same entity. And because of that, you cannot say that one carries more blessings than another; they are all the same in this respect. That is why it is said that if you practise just one deity until you perfect the practice and actually behold the face of the deity, at that point you see the faces of all yidam deities.

Some practitioners request many different empowerments. They receive the empowerments and the various samaya commitments that go with them, they do the various recitation practices associated with them, and thus realize the various profound features of each of them. Despite that, there is no real difference between doing that and requesting and practising one deity.

Why then, if all the deities are one entity from the perspective that they are the luminance of the dharmakaya, were various deities taught? It is because the sentient beings to be tamed through the practice of a yidam deity, the disciples, each have their specific interests and capacities—for example, at the time of practising, each has his own ability to open up to blessings. Thus, various deities with their specific qualities were taught to suit the various disciples with their various capabilities and qualities.

Each of the various yidams belongs to a specific tantra and each tantra belongs to one of four main classes of tantra. The classes of tantra and hence the yidams that go with them suit different individuals. For the person who prefers practice in which ritual activities of cleanliness are foremost, the system of Kriyatantra, that is, Activity Tantra, was taught. In the practice of Kriyatantra, there is a great emphasis on external ritual activities in general and of cleanliness in particular. For example, washing is important and alcohol, meat, and other impure foods are rejected. Some people prefer a practice in which meditative concentration is important; for them, the tantras of the Yogatantra class were taught. Some others have faith in both approaches of ritual activities and of meditative concentration; for them, the tantras of Charyatantra, that is, Conduct Tantra, were taught. Then there are some who are Great Vehicle types but who have very great determination and perseverance, and very strong afflictions; for them, the Unsurpassed Yogatantra was taught.

The Buddha stated that Unsurpassed Yogatantra has the special feature that a practitioner of it can attain buddhahood in one lifetime, in one body. One reason for this is that the system of Unsurpassed Yogatantra has teachings for dealing with the subtle aspects of the body: the channels that the winds travel through and the drops that are situated within them. Specifically, it has methods for removing their impure aspects and returning them to their primordially pure counterparts, which correspond to enlightenment itself.

When we die, the coarse, physical body ends and at the same time, the channels, winds, and drops also end. However, because of karmic habits, they re-appear when we take birth again. These subtle but impure aspects of the body will continually reappear until the karmic habits that cause them have been purified.

In terms of the channels, the human body has one major channel and many subsidiary channels. The subsidiary ones branch out and out from the main one in stages, spreading throughout the body—one thousand and seventy-two of them are counted. In the meditation of a deity's body, only some of these channels are visualized and worked with and they are called "the meditation wind-channels". They are comprised of the main channel which is in the central axis of the body, one major channel to the left of that central channel, and one to the right of it. Then, there are four chakras associated with the central channel. By using the meditation wind-channels in the practices of the yidam deity, in the end all of the channels and winds are purified and, as a result, the actuality of mind, Mahamudra, is brought forth into direct perception.

In fact, there are three main aspects of the subtle body as mentioned above: the channels are a basis through which the winds move and the winds are the carriers of the drops. When we do these practices connected with the subtle body, the channels, winds, and drops all are purified from their impure situation into their primordially pure form. For example, in the case of the winds, they are purified from their impure condition as karmic winds into wisdom winds. The collective final purification of the channels, drops, and winds comes out as the three vajras of enlightenment. The impure channels, winds, and drops purified into pure channels, winds, and drops results in the nirmanakaya, sambhogakaya, and dharmakaya respectively of a buddha.

What is the basis that supports these channels, winds, and drops? It is our impure physical body. Because of grasping at the body, because of the karmic latencies of having a body, because of attachment to a body, and so on, we go through the process of death and then birth in one of the four places of birth and so wander on in samsara. The Buddha taught four different methods within creation stage to purify the four ways of taking birth. Meditation on the first, called The Five Manifest Enlightenments, purifies the habit of birth in the womb; meditation on the second, called The Four Vajras, purifies the habits of birth in an egg; meditation on the third, called The Three Rituals, purifies the habits of birth through heat and moisture; and meditation on the fourth, called Instant of Recollection purifies the habits of birth in a miraculous way.

The grasping, karmic latencies, attachment, and so on that you have in relation to a body will not disappear of themselves. Methods like the ones mentioned must be applied. For example, if you are reborn in the hell realms, you have a kind of body that suffers horribly. It is continually killed and revived only to be killed and revived again. This kind of body comes from karmic latencies of a body created by previous bad deeds. And in dreams you meet various dangers and fears, for example, being at the verge of great abysses, at the mercy of floods, eaten by wild animals, and so on; these dream bodies also come from karmic latencies that were produced by grasping done in relation to a body. And in the intermediate state you develop a subtle body also due to previous karmic latencies. When these karmic latencies have been purified, the karmically produced bodies cease and that is the point of doing these creation stage practices.

At the time of death, the ground luminosity dawns, but if it is not recognized, the person goes on to develop the mental body of an intermediate-state being. However, if a yidam-deity has been practised in the preceding life, it is possible that the lustre of the luminosity will not come out as the mental body of a intermediate-state being, but will come out as the mandala of the yidam-deity, and if

that happens, it is possible that the person could attain enlightenment in the pure realm of the deity.

In the practice of a yidam deity, it is said that one should first do the
visualization by the Instant of Recollection method. In one instant,
just as one thinks of it, the whole visualization—seat, deity, seed
syllables, and so on—appears. This corresponds to, for example,
"In an instant, I appear as the co-emergent Heruka". The effect of
producing the visualization with this method is that it purifies the
karmic latencies of all four places of birth but especially of miraculous birth.

The second style is to produce the visualization with the Three
Rituals. In this, the first ritual is the visualization of the seat; the
second is the visualization of the seed-syllable on the seat; and the
third is the visualization of the deity from that seed-syllable. For
example, "On top of a lotus, from a white HRĪḤ letter, comes
Avalokiteshvara". This method purifies the karmic latencies of all
four kinds of birth place in general and rebirth from heat and
moisture in particular.

The third style is to produce the visualization with The Four
Vajras. In this, the first vajra is to rest in emptiness for a little; the
second is that the seat with seed syllable appears from the emptiness; the third is the visualization of the deity fully complete with
all attributes; and the fourth is the visualization within the deity's
body of the seed syllables at the crown, throat, and heart centre of
enlightened body, speech, and mind and the seed syllable and seat
particular to the deity. This method purifies the karmic latencies
of all four kinds of birth place in general and rebirth in an egg in
particular.

The fourth style is to produce the visualization with The Five
Manifest Enlightenments. In this, the first is to rest in emptiness
for a little; the second is the production from the emptiness of a
seed-syllable and from that a seat; the third is the visualization of

the deity's seed syllable on the seat; and the fourth is the visualization of light radiating out from the seed syllable to accomplish the two purposes of gathering the blessings of all the buddhas and enlightened beings and purifying the evil deeds and obscurations of all sentient beings; and the fifth is the visualization of the seed syllable transforming into the complete deity. For example in the visualization of Tara, "From emptiness a PAM, from that a white lotus, on it a TAM. From it light goes out to all the buddhas and gathers their blessings and to all of the sentient beings and purifies all of their evil deeds and obscurations. TAM transforms into the form of the deity, Tara". This method purifies the karmic latencies of all four birth kinds of birth place in general and rebirth in a womb in particular.

The author of the text that is being commented on here, Zhamarpa Konchog Yanlag, gives the description of the visualization of the deity and recitation, and so on, using the visualization ritual of Chakrasamvara.

The text says, *Meditating on creation stage like that gets to the point concerning desire, will pacify the negative forces of senmo, will bring desire under control, will overpower appearances, and will cause individually discriminating wisdom to dawn. In brief, it is important to work assiduously at creation stage; he said:*

> One's own body is the king of deity forms,
> But if not taken to the firm stage of changeless foundation,
> The dakinis will not assemble into a retinue around it,
> So you must work assiduously at this body, the yidam deity.

The primordial forms of the channels, winds, and drops are within your body, but if you do not practise the method for purifying them, they will not be brought forth. Therefore, you must practise creation stage.

Commentary to the Third of the Five Parts, Guru-yoga

The third of the five parts is guru-yoga meaning unification with the guru. The text says, *The guru is a being inseparable from the wisdom present in every one of the buddhas so one takes the attitude of certainty that he is the embodiment of the three kayas and five wisdoms of a buddha whose inexhaustible sphere of ornamentation of body, speech, mind performs the ripening and liberating of every sentient being until samsara ends.* There are certain attitudes that you need to have in relation to the guru. One is the attitude that your root guru is a being who has become inseparable with the wisdom of the buddhas of the three times and being so is the three kayas and five wisdoms of a buddha embodied, a being who works for the aims of sentient beings in samsara until samsara is emptied.

And, you take the attitude that your own mindness is inseparable from the guru because of which all the dharmas of samsara and nirvana are the nature of appearance and emptiness. This attitude is called "dharmakaya devotion". Resting in equipoise on the guru's mind and your mind being inseparable is called dharmakāya devotion. Having merged your mind with the guru's mind like that, it is possible to take the attitude that all the dharmas of samsara and nirvana are the nature of appearance-emptiness. When you do, you cultivate all visual forms as particulars of the body of the guru, all sounds as the sounds of the guru's speech, and all thoughts as the realization of the guru's mind, the luminous dharmakaya.[106]

It is said that there are many qualified gurus in the world teaching their students but there is only one who actually assists us. This means that there are many gurus in the world with great qualities and meditation experience and that they have their own students whom they are teaching. We cannot meet with all of them and cannot get oral instructions from all of them but we can meet with, obtain instructions from, and practise with some of them. We end up practising with the gurus with whom we have a connection.

There are two types of connection: one is there but not obvious; the other is there and we are aware of it. Sometimes we meet a guru whom we have met and made a relationship with in a past life. The strength of the past connection leads us to a connection again and again in future lives and, when we meet again, the connection is very clear. For example, there is story of Milarepa. His mother had told him to learn black magic and then take revenge on their relatives who had wronged the family. He did that and successfully caused great harm to his relatives. Milarepa eventually had regret for his evil deeds and sought a spiritual teacher who could help him. He found a teacher called Rongtong Lhaga. Rongytong Lhaga gave him the Dzogchen instructions, however, practising the instructions did not have much effect. Rongtong Lhaga told Milarepa that they did not have such a strong connection and that he should go to another teacher with whom he had a stronger connection. He mentioned Marpa of Lhodrak's name and, just on hearing it, Milarepa was immediately overwhelmed with strong feelings and knew that he should meet with Marpa. Milarepa

---

[106] This is the formal way of saying that the practitioner mixes his own mind with the mind of the guru and, as he remains in that state, all appearances are practised as being inseparable appearance-emptiness. Ultimately, just by this kind of devotion, it is possible to go directly to unified appearance-emptiness.

headed off to Lhodrak to find Marpa. Marpa knew that one of his important disciples would be arriving that morning so he took some beer and went down the road to one of his fields, where he started ploughing the field. Milarepa arrived and asked if he knew of Marpa. Marpa did not let on who he was but said to him, "Look, plough this field and have some beer, and I will make arrangements for you to meet Marpa". Milarepa agreed and drank the whole pot of beer in one go. Marpa was very pleased with this because he took it as a sign that in the future Milarepa would be a good vessel for all of the instructions that he could give him. Marpa went off to his house. Sometime later someone else came and took Milarepa up to Marpa's house, then led him inside where Milarepa found that Marpa was none other than the man who had given the beer and asked him to plough the field. Milarepa was overcome with joy and made prostrations. He said to Marpa, "I am a great sinner. Please teach me the dharma and give me food and clothes". Marpa replied that he could do one or the other but not both and asked Milarepa which one he wanted. Milarepa replied that he would learn dharma and find food and clothes in some other way. So if this kind of meeting occurs, it is very clear that the guru and disciple have a very strong connection from the past and that they will probably have the same good connection again in this life.

It was similar with Milarepa and his main student, Gampopa. Gampopa had heard many Kadampa teachings from his Kadampa master, had become a fully ordained monk, and just by hearing instructions on enlightenment mind and emptiness had excellent meditations. One day Gampopa came across three beggars who were discussing Milarepa and his great qualities. When Gampopa heard Milarepa's name, great faith arose in him and later he received all of Milarepa's instructions.

If you meet a qualified guru with special qualities, you must create a connection and request instruction from him. If you do not, as the Buddha said, there is effectively no guru and no instruction, and without instruction it is not possible to practise. He said in the

Condensed Prajñaparamita Sutra that a student who has a good mind and diligence should attend an authentic and learned guru because in reliance on him, all good qualities and realization can arise. Then he said in the *Eight Thousand Verse Prajñaparamita Sutra* that, for those who are oriented towards the attainment of enlightenment, it is necessary to attend and rely on a virtuous spiritual friend.

When you have the kind of faith that the guru is someone who has the activities of a buddha, who actually does liberate sentient beings from unsatisfactoriness, you also see that the guru is as kind as each of the buddhas. It is written in many places that "the guru is the same as buddha" but this instruction is not saying that the guru's qualities are the same as those of a buddha. A supreme nirmana-kaya buddha, a world-leading buddha who performs the twelve acts of enlightenment, and so on, has many special qualities that are not shared by anyone less than a buddha of that level. What it is saying is that the guru and a buddha are the same from the perspective of kindness. The complete true bhagavat buddha, Shakyamuni Buddha, appeared in our world, turned the unfathomable wheel of dharma, and the teaching of the buddhas spread in the world. For us, if there is no guru, we will not be able to obtain the empowerments, transmissions, and special oral instructions needed for practice. Since the guru provides these to us, his kindness is equal to Shakyamuni Buddha's kindness.

In India, the Buddha gave all the dharma teachings, both sutra and tantra, which then flourished. Many generations of beings practised them and attained realization. Having attained realization, they passed the meaning on to other beings who then in turn practised them and realized them. The teachings became a great force in India but all of that was in dependence on the gurus who were kind enough to transmit the teachings. Eventually Tibetans came down to India and obtained the instructions and took them back to Tibet where they were translated into the Tibetan language. These teachings have been practised and realized and transmitted from guru to disciple up to the present day.

In Tibet, there came to be four main lines of transmission of the Buddha's teaching, but they are essentially the same in that all of them pass on the Buddha's teaching. Prior to the seventh century C.E., the Buddha's teaching had not spread in Tibet. Due to the prayers and activities of the buddhas and bodhisatvas, King Songtsen Gampo appeared in Tibet in the early seventh century C.E. and established Buddhism as the state religion of Tibet. About one hundred years later, his descendant King Trisong Deutsen, in order to further the dharma, invited the great guru called Padmasambhava, who later became known in Tibet as the Guru Rinpoche, meaning "The Precious Guru". Guru Rinpoche was especially instrumental in strengthening and spreading the dharma in Tibet and is regarded by Tibetans as the kindest of gurus to have come to Tibet. The teachings imparted by him are maintained in what is called the Nyingma tradition and all schools of the Nyingma regard him as the source guru for their teachings.

In the ninth century, the Tibetan king of the time, called Langdarma, tried very hard to eliminate the Buddhist teachings from Tibet and almost succeeded. Late, in the early eleventh century, there was a revival of Buddhism in Tibet. At the beginning of this revival, the great Indian master Atisha was invited to come from Nalanda monastic university in India to Tibet. He did so and stayed in Tibet for a number of years until his death. The lineage of his teachings became known as the Kadampa tradition and he is regarded as the source guru of those teachings. Later in Tibet in the fifteenth century, an exceptionally brilliant man was born in Amdo. He eventually moved to Lhasa, where he became known as Tsongkhapa. He had over one hundred and fifty gurus, though his principal ones were Kadampa, Sakya, and Kagyu. He established a seat at a place called Ganden Hill and the lineage that developed from him became known as the Gadenpa. They carried on the Kadampa lineage in particular, and later they became known as the Gelugpa. When the followers of the tradition think of their main guru, they look up to Tsongkhapa as the founding guru of the lineage.

In the twelfth century, a man called Drogmi Lotsawa went down to India a number of times where he met the greatly accomplished beings named Gayadhara and Virupa and received all of their instructions. Back in Tibet, he translated and transmitted their teachings which consisted principally of Hevajra tantra and the Path and Fruit teachings. He was located in a place called Sakya so the lineage that developed from him became known as the Sakya lineage. Shortly after him came the main holder and Tibetan source of the lineage The Great Sakya, Kunga Nyingpo. Four other great masters and holders of the lineage following him are grouped with him as the main gurus of the lineage; collectively they are called the Five Sakya Forefathers.

Also in the twelfth century, the translator Marpa went to India and received all the instructions of mahasiddha Naropa. He returned to Tibet and the lineage that developed from him became known as the Kagyu lineage. The Kagyu lineage is considered to start with Tailopa, who passed it to Naropa, then it went to Marpa, then to Milarepa, and then Gampopa. Gampopa's three main, secret mantra disciples were known as the Three Men of Kham, as mentioned earlier. One of them was called "Grey Hair from Kham". He later became known as Dusum Khyenpa, the first Karmapa, and he is considered to be the founder of the Karma Kagyu lineage. The instructions being passed on here are being passed on through that lineage.

Dusum Khyenpa was not an ordinary being. He had already practised for many lifetimes. In a previous lifetime, an incalculable amount of time earlier, there was a king called King Yungkhor Jung who had one thousand sons, the youngest of whom was named Great Being Chokyi Lodro. Great Being Chokyi Lodro found samsara to be hollow and aroused renunciation, developed concentration, and directly perceived reality. He was a holder of the Buddhas' teaching with qualities of great determination and perseverance. All the buddhas empowered him with an empowerment called "the empowerment of the activity of the buddhas". Because of this, he was known afterwards, for example in our world, in his incarnation as Grey Hair from Kham, as "Karmapa" meaning "the one who performs the activities of the buddhas". That great being was praised by many beings, including one hundred thousand dakinis. They each took a hair from their heads and used it to weave a black crown which they then presented to him. The hat is always with him and, if your obscurations have been sufficiently purified, can be seen hovering above his head, it is said. In this world, it is said that he was born in India as the Brahmin called Saraha. Saraha was a greatly accomplished person who continually showed and taught Mahamudra. This was mentioned by All-Knowing Longchen Rabjam's biography when it says, "The great siddha Saraha of India, in his later rebirth as the third Karmapa, Karmapa Rangjung Dorje ..." Then, at the time of Guru Rinpoche, it is said that Karmapa was one of the twenty-five principal disciples of Guru Rinpoche, a being called Gyalwa Chowang. Later still, he became Grey Hair from Kham, as mentioned above. Karmapa is regarded as the founding father of the Karma Kagyu lineage.

Within the Kagyu lineage there are the four great and eight lesser schools of the Kagyu. The four greater ones derive from four principal disciples of Gampopa and the eight lesser ones derive from principal disciples of Phagmo Drupa. Each of these traditions looks to the founder of its lineage as the most important guru of the lineage. For example, Jigten Sumgon is the founder of the Drigung Kagyu and most important guru for that lineage and Tsangpa Gyare, in his incarnations as the Drukchen, is the most important guru for the Drukpa Kagyu tradition.

Thus, followers of the Karma Kagyu will visualize Karmapa when they do this practice of guru-yoga or do other practices where the principal guru of the lineage must be meditated on. The text gives the following instructions for doing the visualization for practising guru-yoga: *For the purpose of making a visualization of the guru, do this. Above the crown of yourself clearly seen as the deity, in space, on a lion throne, on a seat of lotus and moon, the root guru appears in the form which is the embodiment of the Jewels, the summation of the families, Vajradhara. He has a blue body, one face, and two arms, and holds a vajra and bell crossed at his heart. He is adorned with various jewelled ornaments and wears the silken pants. His feet are crossed in vajrasana. He has a peaceful mood and is surrounded by the lineage gurus, the deity assemblies of the yidam mandalas, and the dharmapalas and guards.* Thus, on top of your head, on a throne supported by eight lions, on a thousand-petalled lotus, on a sun seat, and on a moon seat on top of that, sits the Karmapa, appearing in the form of dharmakaya Vajradhara, holding vajra and bell crossed in front of his chest, and seated in vajra posture. Above him all the lineage gurus, Tailopa, Naropa, Marpa, and so on, are actually present. In front of him, all the yidams of the Kagyu tradition—Chakrasamvara and so on—are actually present. Below him, all of the dharmapalas and guards of the lineage, such as Mahakala are actually present. This instruction is not the same as the usual one for the preliminary practices. It is a special instruction of the Five-Part Mahamudra lineage.

Then, supplicate: "Glorious guru great Vajradhara, please bless my body, speech, and mind, all three." Here, followers of the Karma Kagyu would pray using the words "Karmapa khyen no" or "Karmapa know me", which have the same meaning in this context as, "Karmapa, we take refuge in you".

Because of that, white, red, and blue light spring one after the other from the crown, throat, and heart-centre of Vajradhara. In sequence, they dissolve into my own three places, purifying the obscurations of the three doors. Meditate on the thought that you have been made into a fortunate one whose ordinary body, speech, and mind have been manifested as the vajras of enlightened body, speech, and mind. Then, having supplicated Karmapa like that, think that white light radiates from Karmapa's forehead and dissolves into your crown. "All the evil deeds and obscurations of body have been purified. The blessings of Karmapa's enlightened body have been received". Then think that red light radiates from Karmapa's throat and dissolves into your throat.

"All the evil deeds and obscurations of speech have been purified. The blessings of Karmapa's enlightened speech have been received". Then think that blue light radiates from Karmapa's heart centre and dissolves into your heart centre. "All the evil deeds and obscurations of mind have been purified. The blessings of Karmapa's enlightened mind have been received". Then think that white, red, and blue lights simultaneously radiate from Karmapa's forehead, throat, and heart centre and dissolve into your three places. "All the combined evil deeds and obscurations of the three doors altogether have been purified. The blessings of Mahamudra have been received".

At the close of the session, the retinue dissolves into guru Vajradhara. Then he dissolves into you and your ordinary person now becomes the guru's enlightened body, speech, and mind inseparable with your own body, speech, and mind. The lineage gurus above guru Vajradhara first melt into light and dissolve into him. Then the yidams in front melt into light and dissolve into him. Then the dharmapalas and guards below melt into light and dissolve into him. Finally, the guru melts into light then dissolves into you, his mind merges with yours, and you rest equipoised in the actuality of mind directly manifest.

Meditating on guru-yoga like that gets to the point concerning pride ... in other words, from among the five afflictions, it becomes an antidote to pride ... *will pacify the negative force of devaputra, will bring prideful states under control, will give you the ability to bless others* ... It will give you the capability of blessing others ... *and will cause the wisdom of equality to dawn* ... in other words, from among the five wisdoms, the wisdom of equality will dawn. *In brief, it is important to work assiduously at guru-yoga; he said:*

> *If the sun of devotion does not shine*
> *On the snow mountain of the guru's four kayas,*
> *The stream of blessings will not descend,*
> *So work assiduously at devotion.*

He likens the four enlightened kayas of the guru to a snow mountain and says that, unless the sunshine of devotion falls upon on that snow mountain, it will not melt and the stream of blessings will not descend, hence it is important to work assiduously at devotion.

Commentary to the Fourth of the Five Parts, Mahamudra

The fourth oral instruction of the Five Parts is Mahamudra. The explanation of Mahamudra contains three topics: ground Mahamudra, path Mahamudra, and fruition Mahamudra.

Mahamudra is a name that refers to reality. Reality is present in your mindstream as its basis. That is the ground Mahamudra. Even though it is present in you, it is obscured and has to be brought out, manifested. The way for it to be brought out is called path Mahamudra. When it is finally and fully manifested by practising the path, you become buddha and that is called fruition Mahamudra.

In order to tread the path of Mahamudra, you have to do the meditation practice of Mahamudra. However, to do that, you first have to determine the view of Mahamudra. In other words, you first have to come to a clear understanding of ground Mahamudra then it will be possible for your meditation practice to bring the ground Mahamudra into manifestation. The view of Mahamudra is obtained by looking into the situation of mind and its actuality.

In regard to this, the text says, *The way that mindness is present within you is not known by the rational mind of samsara and nirvana.* The mindness of Mahamudra comes out into appearance in one of two ways, which we call samsara and nirvana. When it appears as

samsara, it comes out as the appearances of the six types of migrators and the sufferings that they experience. In this case, appearances are the results of karma and latencies that were previously
produced by evil deeds and obscurations. If these apparent beings
of samsara practise the path, they go from the side of samsara to the
side of nirvana. When the mindness of Mahamudra appears as
nirvana, it comes out as the buddhas with all of their qualities—
body, speech, mind, qualities, actions, and so on. In this way, the
text teaches that all of the different appearances, those of samsara
and those of nirvana, come from the one source; all are appearances
coming from mindness.

All sentient beings have a mind and they also have an essence of
that mind. For all of them, the confusion that they experience
comes about only in mind; for all of them, the essence of mind itself
never changes, never becomes confused. This essence of mind
itself has two main aspects—an entity of emptiness and a nature of
luminosity—and these two aspects are primordially unified. When
confusion occurs, the luminosity becomes ignorant of the unification of the two and a style of grasping at appearances as other than
itself develops, producing a sense of this and that. Following that,
a style of grasping at a solidified self on the basis of the empty factor
happens. The confusion over appearances of the luminosity
becomes the basis for anger and envy and the confusion over the
emptiness, the confusion of grasping at a solidified self, becomes
the basis for the afflictions of desire and jealousy. On the basis of
this ignorance and the afflictions arising from it, karma is accumulated and adventitious obscurations appear. Mind's essence does
not have obscurations intrinsic to it, nevertheless the process of
ignorance, karma, and afflictions that has come about is a kind of
dualistic movement of mind that has various sorts of adventitious
obscurations with it[107]. These obscurations cause sentient beings to

---

[107] Tib. glo bur gyi dri ma. "Adventitious obscurations" are the
(continued ...)

wander through the six types of becoming and experience the various types of unsatisfactoriness that go with them. In this way, the entirety of the unsatisfactoriness of samsara happens as an appearance of mind.

If you practise the path of profound meditation, the adventitious obscurations will be gradually cleared off and the good qualities of the paths and stages will appear as you progress through the bodhisatva levels. In the final analysis, the good qualities of realization of the paths and levels that come from the removal of the adventitious obscurations by practising the path and all the good qualities of buddhahood are things that occur only on the basis of mind. Thus, all of the things of nirvana also only come about as appearances of mind.

The text says, *It is not known through the exaggerations of appearance and emptiness. It is not the experience of appearance. It is not the experience of emptiness.* When considering the mindness which is Mahamudra and trying to determine what it is, you might say that it was just the appearance part, the luminosity aspect of mind's essence alone, and that there is no emptiness aspect associated with it, but it is not like that. The luminosity aspect does come out into appearance as all the phenomena of samsara and nirvana, but that luminosity aspect is primordially unified with the emptiness aspect—it is not something separate and off by itself.

Similarly, you might think that mindness which is Mahamudra is an emptiness that is a non-existence like the horns of a rabbit, something that has no function, but it is also not like that, for it has an entity of an empty condition but also has a nature of luminosity because of which all the appearances of samsara and nirvana can

---

[107] (... continued)
movements of dualistic mind that suddenly appear on the surface of the mindness or mind's essence. They do indeed obscure it, but are not part of it, so can be eliminated.

appear, all of the pleasures and pains of samsara can be experienced, and that is how it is directly known.

The text says, *It is not the experience of existence. It is not the experience of non-existence.* If you were to identify mind as an actual thing that existed, that would not be right. If it were that way, then it would have some particular characteristic known to the senses such as visual colour and shape. However, even the buddhas have not seen a mind having colour, shape, or other characteristic. Thus, it is not an existent thing. Similarly, it is not a non-existent thing, for it is the basis of everything in samsara and nirvana.

The text says, *It is not the experience of confusion. It is not the experience of liberation. It is beyond every one of these biassed positions, all of which are falls to one side or another.* Sentient beings are confused. When they totally clear off their adventitious obscurations, they become liberated as buddhas with all of the various buddha-qualities. In doing so, they do not improve the mind and make it better. Rather, they remove the obscurations that were covering mind's essence and, just by doing that, reveal the dharmakaya with all of its buddha-qualities. Thus, when a being becomes a buddha, mind's essence does not change or become better. Similarly, when beings fall into the various states of samsara—for example into the hell realms—with the various attendant experiences of suffering, it is not that the minds of the beings have developed some bad qualities and become worse than before. Rather, the essence of mind of those beings has become obscured and, having become obscured, it manufactures the suffering appearances of samsara experienced by the beings. Thus, when a being falls into samsara, the essence of mind does not change or become worse. Overall, the essence of mind does not ever become better or worse as it experiences samsara and nirvana.

The Buddha spoke of this essence of mind which is unified emp
tiness-appearance as "the lineage element tathagatagarbha"[108] because it is the enlightened lineage present in all sentient beings and
is the element or core of mind that is the progenitor of becoming
a tathagata. All of us do have this element, therefore, it is possible
for us to become buddhas. The Buddha did not say that just
because we have the tathagatagarbha within us we are buddhas. He
said that we have it but only as the potential for future enlightenment. He said that this potential can be cleansed through the
practice of meditation and that will reveal the mind of a buddha.
He said that to be able to do that, it is necessary to take birth not
just in any human body but in the excellent type of human body
called a precious human body. Moreover, just having a precious
human body is not sufficient; it is then necessary on top of that to
find a virtuous spiritual friend and connect with him. And just
finding and being with such a spiritual friend is not enough, it is
also necessary to receive instruction from him. Even that is not
enough; it is necessary to take those instructions and practise them
and through that it will be possible, because of the cause, the
lineage element, that is present in the practitioner's mind, to
become a buddha.

The text says, *The actuality that is the way that your innate disposition
is present is called "Ground Mahamudra"*. At first, in order to explain
the meditation of Mahamudra, there is an explanation of the
ground reality as just given. It is about the actuality of mind that is
the essence of mind, which is unified emptiness-appearance, which
is the basis from which the two types of appearance—the appearances of samsara and of nirvana—come, which is the cause present
in all beings called tathagatagarbha that allows sentient beings to
become buddha if they practise the path. That is called Ground
Mahamudra.

---

[108] "The lineage element tathagatagarbha" is a longer way of saying
"buddha nature".

You need to develop a correct understanding of this ground Mahamudra and, if you do, that will be called "the view of Mahamudra".
However, just having the view is not sufficient. Until ground
Mahamudra has been fully manifested in your being, that is, until
it has been fully realized, it is necessary to practise meditation in
order to manifest it, to realize it. The meditation practice needed
to realize it involves two practices: calm-abiding and insight also
known by their Sanskrit names, shamatha and vipashyana respectively. As the text says, *The way of meditating on it has two parts:
calm-abiding and insight.*

1. Calm Abiding

The text says, *There are three parts to this: holding where there is no
holding; steadying of the holding; and ways of improving the steadiness.*

In order to do the calm-abiding meditation, the body is placed in a
particular posture called the "Seven Points of Vairochana". The
posture is important because it creates a foundation for the calm-
abiding practice. Not being able to assume the posture does not
mean that you cannot do the practice. For instance, if you have
some sickness or disability that prevents you from sitting in the
posture, sit in the posture to the extent that you can, otherwise
simply take a posture that is comfortable and do the practice like
that.

The text says, *The legs are crossed up. With the hands in the equipoise
mudra, the shoulders are opened, the spine is straightened, the chin is
hooked in a little, the lips and teeth are left to sit in their own way, and
the gaze is directed down the tip of the nose, directly ahead into space.*
The posture for the legs is the one called "vajrasana" in Sanskrit
meaning "vajra posture". In it, the legs are crossed one on top of
the other, right on top of left. The advantage of this posture is that,
of the five basic winds of the subtle body, the downward-clearing
wind is caused to enter the central channel. The posture for the
hands is called the equipoise mudra. The right palm is placed on

top of the left palm and the two thumbs are just touching, raised up over the palms. The advantage of this posture is that the Fire-Accompanying Wind is caused to enter the central channel. The posture for the spine is that the spine should be held straight. The advantage of this posture is that the Pervader Wind is caused to enter the central channel. The posture for the shoulders is one in which the shoulders are held open in a particular way. The advantage of this posture is that Upward-Moving Wind is caused to enter the central channel. The neck and chin are held in a particular posture: the neck is drawn up a little and the chin slightly hooked in towards the throat. The advantage of this posture is that the Life-Holder Wind is caused to enter the central channel. The tip of the tongue is joined with the forward part of the palate and the jaws are relaxed, with the teeth and lips allowed to sit normally. The eyes are directed down past the tip of the nose, into space. Placing the gaze in this way keeps the luminosity of mind and prevents sinking, agitation, and so on.

The text says, *Having done that, the mind is left in its natural condition.* Now that the body has been set into the appropriate posture, set your mind into equipoise without the use of an object of meditation—set it into equipoise on emptiness. This is calm-abiding meditation because you are setting the mind in one place and, since it is done without a specific object that the mind is being set on, it is calm-abiding without a referenced object.

The point of calm-abiding meditation is to develop an abiding mind, a mind that does not have any mental proliferation occurring within it. If, when you do calm-abiding in the way just mentioned—using emptiness as the basis for the resting—no discursive thoughts appear, then it means that you are staying in what is called "abiding". If, on the other hand, discursive thoughts pop up, then the abiding has been pushed out of the way and replaced by what is called "movement". When practising calm-abiding, if movement occurs, it is necessary to stop the movement, that is, the discursive thoughts, and return to the abiding. By practising this way, you develop an abiding that is increasingly steady.

In general, it is said that beginners who practise Mahamudra meditation should do "short sessions many times". It is said that if you meditate on the actuality of mind in this way, then you will slowly attain stability in the meditation and eventually great qualities will come because of it.

The text says, *If the mind will not abide when that is done, follow what was is explained in the King of Samadhis Sutra:*

> *The body like the colour of gold,*
> *The protector of the world, more beautiful than all—*
> *Whatever mental placement is done with that as the support*
> *The bodhisatva calls "equipoise".*

For that, visualize in front of you, on a lion throne, on a seat of lotus and moon, the truly complete Buddha's form and, setting the mind one-pointedly on it, do not be distracted from that object of visualization to something else.

The *King of Samadhis Sutra* is a sutra of the Buddha. The first two lines of the verse just quoted refer to the kind of body that the Buddha had, with the thirty-two marks and eighty insignia and so on. If a person were to meditate using that kind of golden body as an object of the calm-abiding meditation then, as it says, a bodhisatva would regard that as what is called "equipoise". To meditate in this way, visualise before you a throne supported by eight lions, with a lotus on top, with a moon disk on top of that, and Buddha Shakyamuni on top of that. His body is the colour of refined gold. He has one face and two arms, with the right-hand placed in the earth-touching mudra and the left in equipoise mudra. He wears the three dharma robes and his feet are drawn up into full lotus position. You should especially place your attention on the heart-centre of the visualization.

The text says, *When doing that, if sinking-dullness occurs, move your mental focus to the topknot and if agitation-excitement occurs, move your mental focus to the seat.* When doing this kind of meditation, if sinking-dullness of any kind happens, you shift your attention to the crown protuberance of the visualised Buddha and meditate with your mind there. On the other hand, if the mind becomes stirred up and gives off many thoughts or very intense ones, you shift your attention to the lotus seat and meditate with your mind there.

Another way to practise calm-abiding meditation is to use the breath as the object of the meditation. When doing calm-abiding this way, the breath is allowed to go out and come in as it normally would without any alteration to the breathing pattern. In general, the attention is focussed on the sensation of the breath going in and out at the tip of the nose. However, in this kind of meditation, it is also possible to practise using the movement of the breath through each of the right and left nostrils. The movement of breath through the right nostril is connected with the movement of the winds of the right channel called "the sun winds of prajña". The movement of breath through the left nostril is connected with the movement of the winds of the left channel called "the moon winds of method". Through these practices you eventually gain control over the moon-like left-channel winds and the sun-like right channel winds. At that time, the respective winds are captured and inserted into the central channel.

When the moon-like winds are captured and brought into the central channel, the practitioner gains control over the five sense faculties. For example, a practitioner who has control over the sense faculties in this way could look at something such as a flower and by moving the eyes could cause the flower to move with the gaze. In a similar way, control is obtained over the other four senses: distant sounds can be heard by the ears; distant smells can be smelled by the nose; tastes can be changed from one to another by the tongue, such as sweet to astringent, and so on; and the sensations of the body can be changed from one to another such as cold to hot, and so on. There is a story about the greatly accomplished Indian named Krishna, a Chakrasamvara yogin, that illustrates this. Krishna came across an orchard guarded by a young woman. He asked for some fruit but she replied, "If you are a yogin with attainment, then bring the fruit down yourself and then you can have it". So he put his gaze on the fruit, moved his eyes downwards, and the fruit fell to the ground. However, she then put her gaze on the fruit, moved her eyes upwards, and the fruit went back onto the trees!

When the sun-like winds are captured and brought into the central channel, the practitioner gains three qualities. When the sun winds are captured, then the moon winds of the left side and the Rahula winds of the centre are also captured and brought into the central channel. When all three sets of winds have been brought into the central channel, the three poisons of the mind are controlled, reduced, and finally eliminated. Bringing the winds of the right channel into the central channel brings control over anger; bringing the winds of the left channel into the central channel brings control over desire; and bringing the central winds into the central channel brings control over delusion. This is said to be a special method for gaining control over the discursive thoughts of the afflictions.

An effect of doing calm-abiding meditation using the breath as the object is that the winds of the body in general are brought into harmony. When the winds are brought into harmony, then, for the body, various types of sicknesses cannot arise and certain kinds of sicknesses, even though they arise, will be alleviated or at least reduced. In addition to this, for the mind, since the activity of mind is based on the movement of the winds, the various experiences of mind such as suffering, fear, unhappiness, and so on, will be reduced or will not happen. Overall, it is said that calm-abiding meditation using the breath has many advantages.

In the above, three ways of doing calm-abiding meditation have been explained: without an object; using the Buddha's form as an object; and using the breath as an object. It is not necessary to do all three of these, rather, find the one that you are comfortable with and use that.

B. Insight, The Introduction

Generally speaking, it is said that those who have been able, in previous lives, to enter the path in general, then to meet the path of blessings, and within that to accumulate merit and purify evil deeds and obscurations, and so become a mantra holder, can in this life be divided into two types: sudden and gradual. The sudden type of person, even though he does not practise calm-abiding meditation over and over again, can, on the basis of the guru's blessings and also sometimes at the time of the four empowerments, be introduced to the actuality of mind and realize it automatically. For this type of person, not practising calm-abiding over a long period but starting out immediately with training in insight into the actuality of mind is all right. The gradual type of person first meditates over and again on calm-abiding then, once he has some stability in that, moves to insight and is given the introduction; doing it this way makes it is easy for him to realize insight, that is, to receive the introduction.

Why is it necessary for the gradual type to practise calm-abiding in order to gain the insight that comes with the introduction? Because for him, discursive thoughts occur in an uninterrupted stream, like the waves on a lake and this stream of discursive thought partially obscures the essence of mind. The analogy given for this is that, when the surface of a lake is disturbed by waves, it is not possible to see the rocks and other features of the lake-bottom, however, when the waves subside, the bottom can be clearly seen.

The first part of this section of the text shows how insight is imparted to the disciple in the form of an introduction to the nature or essence of the disciple's mind.

The words that show how to give the introduction start with, *When you are abiding one-pointedly in a concentrated state, investigate to see just exactly how is it with this mind that is abiding. What kind of colour does it have while abiding? What kind of shape does it have while abiding?* According to the Five Parts instruction, you first supplicate for the guru's blessings, then take the four empowerments from the guru, then at the end of that, the guru dissolves into you and your mind mixes with the guru's mind, and finally you rest one-pointedly in that state of mind. Now, while you have that abiding on mind, you examine the abiding mind itself to see whether there is some colour to it or not. If you cannot see any kind of colour to that abiding mind, well, then you examine it to see what kind of shape—for example, a square shape, and so on—it has. Now, you won't see any colour or shape to the abiding mind, so when you do not see it, meditate by resting in the equipoise of just that not seeing.

The text says, *The thought, "Well, if I don't see how it is when abiding, then I should look at it when it is proliferating" itself is a proliferation too.* Then, a discursive thought will arise while you are abiding in that equipoise of not seeing any shape or colour in the abiding mind. So now, examine that discursive thought to see whether it has any colour or shape to it. Then, if you do not see any colour or shape to it, rest right on that discursive thought that thinks, "I do not see it".

While meditating that way, if you cannot get the point of the abiding mind and the moving mind and so cannot settle into an actual equipoise as mentioned above, then over and over again: offer a mandala to the guru, supplicate for his blessings, take the four empowerments, then meditate on the actuality of mind.

The text says, *Think strongly, "If I do not recognize the essence of mind, I will not be liberated from existence. If I am not liberated from that, the unsatisfactoriness of birth, old age, sickness, and death will be unbearable. Therefore, I will work only at gaining certainty in the recognition of mind"*. Think like this, "If I do not meet with the actuality of mind, then I will not be able to liberate myself from samsara. If I am not able to liberate myself from samsara, I will not be able to emancipate myself from its sufferings. Therefore I will meditate again and again on the actuality of mind."

The text says, *At all times exert yourself only at staring directly at your own mind; if you do, then you will definitely see it, whatever it is.* When we speak of meditating on Mahamudra, there is no other meditation to do except this: look back this way[109] at your own mind again and again. As Karmapa III, Rangjung Dorje said in his *Prayer of Aspiration to Mahamudra*:

> When looking repeatedly at the mind that cannot be
>   viewed,
> The fact that cannot be seen stands out, vividly.
> Cutting off doubts about whether the ultimate nature is
>   like this or that,
> May you recognise your own face un-erringly.

The object you look at, the mind, has no colour, shape, and so on. Even though there is nothing to be looked at, by using your own self-knowing knower and looking with that again and again, it turns out that what you look at has no colour, shape, and so on, yet can definitely be seen, standing out vividly. If you do meditation like this on the actuality of mind and end up having thoughts like, "Is this it? Maybe this isn't it? I think this is it. I don't think this is it!" then this vacillation back and forth as it is called is a sign that you have not truly seen it. If you truly see the actuality of mind, at that time you exit the realm of doubt.

---

[109] Instead of looking outward at dualistic appearances as mind usually does, you must look towards yourself, towards your actual being.

The greatly accomplished Tailopa said:

> Co-emergence, innate wisdom,
> Dwells at the essence of all migrators,
> But cannot be realized unless shown by the guru;
> Like the oil in sesame seeds is not seen without
>   pounding.

Co-emergent wisdom is present in the mind of every sentient being. However, to realize it, it is necessary first to be introduced to it by the guru and then to realize it by practising guru-yoga and the path of secret mantra, all of which is done on the basis of the guru. Except for that, there is no way to realize it. For example, there is oil within sesame seeds that oil cannot be seen, cannot be obtained, unless the sesame seeds are pounded.

Jamgon Kòngtrul Lodro Thaye also spoke of the way of doing this meditation in *The Lamp of Certainty of Mahamudra*, a text which has been translated into English. He said, "When meditating on the actuality of mind, abide without traces of the past", meaning that it is not necessary to think of the things that have been done in the past, for instance what you did just now, or yesterday, or one week ago, one month ago, one year ago, and so on. Then he said, "Abide without traces of the future" meaning that it is not necessary to think, "I need to do this, I need to do that, one month from now I need to do this, one year from now I will have to do this", and so on. Then he said, "Put yourself in your natural condition in the present consciousness", meaning that you should place yourself in your current consciousness in its natural condition, just as it is, without any construction or alteration of it. Then, having set yourself that way, at some point a discursive thought will suddenly flash out from the equipoise, so he says, "Look penetratingly at the discursive thought itself". Then he says, "It is also not necessary to stop the discursive thought or to follow after it". Thinking, "This discursive thought is an obstacle, an interruption to my abiding", and therefore attempting to stop the thought is unnecessary.

Similarly, you should not follow after the thought because that would just produce more thoughts.

Then, many of the mind instruction texts in the Mahamudra system explain the meditation technique called "the three: abiding, moving, and knowing". "Abiding" refers to meditating with the mind abiding free of discursive thought and with this, it is necessary to know that the mind is actually abiding. Then, from within this state of abiding, discursive thoughts will stir and that is called "movement". Again, when a discursive thought arises like this and the mind is moving, it is also necessary to know that it is that way. Thus, at the time of abiding there is abiding and one knows that mind is abiding and at the time of movement there is movement and one knows that mind is moving. Therefore, from this perspective, Mahamudra meditation is called "threefold abiding, moving, and knowing".

The previous Dudjom Rinpoche, Jigdrel Yeshe Dorje, wrote a text called *Mountain Dharma, Alchemy of Accomplishment*"[110] on mountain dharma, meaning the sort of dharma that goes with being in retreat in an isolated place In it, he said, "If all the meanings of sutra and tantra are rolled up into one and explained ..." meaning that there are many techniques of meditation but if all them are summed up into one and the meaning is shown, it is like this: "When past thoughts have ceased and future thoughts have not yet appeared, if you place yourself in a natural way in the actuality of mind, then there is something there that is clearly knowing, an awareness which is nakedly and distinctly evident, isn't there?!" And when you have placed yourself in a natural way in that clear-empty state, he says, "At that time of no discursive thought, just exactly that itself is rigpa's way of being." In other words, you are staying within

---

[110] *The Dzogchen Alchemy of Accomplishment, Heart Guidance on the Practice Expressed in An Easy-to-understand Way*, book by Tony Duff, published by Padma Karpo Translation Committee, ISBN 978-9937-903-13-4.

the un-contrived actuality of mind. He continues, "Now that abiding will turn into non-authentic abiding, that is, a discursive thought will suddenly flash out from within it" meaning that you will not be able to stay permanently in a true abiding but at some point discursive thoughts will appear. He says, "That is the rigpa's naturally-occurring luminosity" in other words, that is the luminosity of the rigpa itself. He continues, "Discursive thoughts are allowed to arise and, except for just recognizing them, do not create further traces. If they are left recognized right on themselves, then discursive thoughts will wander about in liberation into the open space of dharmakaya". With that he means that there is nothing else to do when discursive thoughts arise but to recognize them and then, having looked at them, rest in just that. If you do it that way, one discursive thought will not lead onto another one, creating further traces. If you do it that way over and again, discursive thoughts will go on to be liberated into dharmakaya. He goes on to say, "If you meditate like that, it is exactly the single instruction of the Great Completion. It is the main practice, that of view and meditation combined into one".

Then also, the great practitioner from the Karma Kamtsang lineage, Khenpo Tashi Ozer, said:

> Since this is the root of meditation
> Look at mind with mind!

That means: "The root of all our meditations is this Mahamudra meditation. How does one do Mahamudra meditation? You have to look at mind with mind". Then he said:

> When mind looks at mind,
> If there is nothing whatsoever to be seen,
> Then meditate in that state!

That means: "When mind looks at mind there is no sensory characteristic—no colour, shape, and so on—to be seen, so if you see nothing, then you must rest in equipoise on that state". Then he said:

> If a blizzard of different thoughts appears
> Look hither at the essence of the thinking!
> If past thoughts have dissolved,
> Then rest in that essence!

That means: "Sometimes many different discursive thoughts will rise and when that happens look right at them. When you do that, they will dissolve away. When they have, meditate in equipoise on that".

That is the way to meditate on Mahamudra. For myself, I think that the practise is fairly easy when you do it by following what the forefather gurus have said and join that with the thought of all sentient beings. You do, however, need perseverance. You do need to meditate on it again and again. You cannot realize Mahamudra through intellectual understanding alone, so you must apply yourself to the practice. Having obtained the instructions on it, you must practise, at least a little.

Generally speaking, there are many different oral instructions from the forefathers of the past. However, even though their names might be different, the meditation that they point at is the same. There is a teaching that says:

> Co-emergence; Amulet Box;
> Five Parts; Equalization of Taste; Four Letters;
> The Pacifier, Cutting; Great Completion;
> Middle Way Instruction on the View; and so on—
> There are many, each with their own name, but
> Their key points, scriptures, and reasonings
> Are just differing circumstances, and these are
> Understood by an experienced yogi as the same.

Gampopa's instructions on Mahamudra, as passed on from the Indian tradition, in general are called *Co-emergence*. Khyungpo Naljor was a great master who went to India, where he stayed for a long time and received all the instructions of Niguma and the greatly accomplished Sukhasiddhi, which were later distilled into a text called *Mahamudra's Amulet Box*, which belongs to the Shangpa Kagyu tradition. Gampopa's disciple Phagmo Drupa gave his disciple Drigung Kyobpa Jigten Sumgon the instruction on the Five Parts, which was later recorded in the text being explained here, *The Source of the Jewels of Experience and Realization, The Ocean-Like Instructions on the Five Parts*. Phagmo Drupa gave his disciple Lingje Repa the Mahamudra instruction called "Equalization of Taste" then he passed it to his principal disciple Tsangpa Gyare, the first incarnation of the Drukchen incarnations of the Drukpa Kagyu. Milarepa's principal disciple Rechungpa went to India and requested many teachings which were later collected together into what became known as "The Rechung Hearing Lineage texts", one of which was called *The Four Letters of Mahamudra*. The Indian master Phadampa Sangyay obtained the instructions of one hundred and fifty Indian masters and later went to Tibet three times; within Tibet, his instructions became known as "The Pacifier, Cutting". Guru Rinpoche went to Tibet at the request of King Trisong Deutsen; his special instructions became known in Tibet as "The Great Completion". The noble ones Nagarjuna and Asanga and the others in their lineages gave rise to the system of "The Great Middle Way" concerning which there are many texts such as a collection of texts called *The Collection of Reasoning*. Thus there are many, differing, names for the dharma that has come through these systems. However, an expert yogin—meaning one who is expert in the sense of having actual experience of the meaning through meditation—who examines their key points, scriptures, and reasonings will see that they all have the same intent. He will know that one is not better or worse than the others, and that none of them contradicts the others.

There is a text that presents the view and practice of the meditation that is special to the Great Completion tradition. It was written by Dza Patrul and is called *Feature of the Expert, Glorious King*, though it is commonly known as *Three Phrases That Hit The Key Points*[111]. The text explains the practice by expanding on three phrases that were spoken by the first human of the Great Completion lineage, Vidyadhara Garab Dorje. Garab Dorje, at the time of going to nirvana, returned from death and appeared in a mass of light to his primcipal disciple Mañjushrimitra. He spoke the three phrases as oral instructions for his disciple and these have been kept as special oral instructions for the practice of Great Completion.

The first of Garab Dorje's three lines was "Recognition based on oneself" and *Three Phrases That Hit The Key Points* expands on it with:

> Nothing whatsoever blankness;
> Blankness has full-view transparency;
> The transparency's inexpressible.
> Identify the rigpa dharmakāya!

"Nothing whatsoever blankness" refers to leaving the mind in its natural condition in the state in which, since all past and future discursive thoughts have stopped, there is nothing at all. Then,"full-view transparency" means that there is unobstructed knowing". Then, "The transparence's inexpressible" means that when you are resting in your natural condition in that state, there is no way that you could describe the state to others using words. Then, "Identify the dharmakāya rigpa", means that you should take that empty blankness that has transparency in which the two together are inexpressible as the thing to be meditated on when meditating on the mindness.

The second of Garab Dorje's three phrases was "Decision on one" and the *Feature of the Expert, Glorious King* expands on it with:

---

[111] *The Feature of the Expert, Glorious King,* book by Tony Duff, published by Padma Karpo Translation Committee, ISBN: 978-9937-824-43-9.

After that, whether it proliferates or dwells is fine ...
At all times and in every circumstance ...
Preserve it as only the shifting events of the dharmakāya.
Make a decision that there is nothing other than that.

Sometimes very strong anger comes to us. Still, it should be brought to the path by putting it into the expanse of meditation. Similarly, no matter what affliction arises, no matter what discursive thought arises—pride, jealousy, passion—it should be carried onto the path by putting it into the state. You might think, for example, "Well, if very strong anger arises, how is that carried into the state of meditation?" To that, Dza Patrul says elsewhere that you should always maintain virtue in relation to the other. In the case of anger, you do not follow the thought and get involved in fights either physically or verbally, and so on. Instead, if the angry thought is allowed to remain in the state, as it is called, of the practice, it will subside itself into what it actually is, mirror-like wisdom. Similarly for desire, pride, jealousy, and so on—all of them are treated in the same way and return to their own wisdoms in the same way.

Now when you are practising this way, sometimes happy or good circumstances will arise. The discursive thought associated with that, of happiness, and so on, should also be dealt with in the same way; it should be brought onto the path by putting it into the state. At times, unpleasant or suffering experiences will happen. For example, the body will become ill or sometimes relatives or friends will have problems and you will suffer because of it; there are many kinds of suffering like this. When that happens, the concepts of the suffering should be mixed in with and made one with the state of practice. By putting them into the equipoise of practice like that, you carry them into the dharmakāya.

Then there are the last two lines of *Feature of the Expert, Glorious King*:

Preserve it as only shifting events of the dharmakāya.
Decide that there is nothing other than that.

All of the various afflictions and sufferings that arise in mind come
from the confused aspect of mind. If they are purified using the
antidote of meditation on Mahamudra or Great Completion, then
they are carried into the path and turned into the dharmakaya, and
no other method is needed to deal with them at all. It is necessary
to decide firmly that that is so and then follow that decision.

The third of Garab Dorje's three phrases was "Assurance built on
liberation" and the *Three Phrases That Hit The Key Points* expands on
it with:

> Every single one of the adventitious discursive thoughts
> Are self-recognized and in the state have no ensuing
>   trace ...
> The way of shining forth being like before compared to
> The way of liberation being distinct is a major key point.

No matter what adventitious discursive thought arises, it is self-
recognized and simultaneously goes on to liberation. In that case,
no karma is accumulated and the thought does not proliferate into
a second thought. In this way of practice, the way that discursive
thoughts arise is the same for the practitioner as for all other
sentient beings. However, there is one very big difference: for the
person who understands how to liberate thoughts, the way it
happens is very different from the way thoughts subside for ordinary beings. For the practitioner, thoughts arise but, together with
their arising, go on to liberation and that is the difference.

Then the greatly accomplished one Saraha said:

> If you rest in uncontrived freshness, realization pervades;
> If you train in a continuous stream, it will appear
>   constantly.
> Totally abandoning every logic that depends on
>   reference

Perpetually rest in equipose, Oh yogin!

This has the following meaning. When you meditate on Mahamudra you need to be without hopes that "My meditation will be a good meditation; I need that" and similarly without fears that "My meditation is not correct, I am following the wrong path". If you rest in your natural condition free from hope and fear, free from needs for success and non-failure, then you will be in uncontrived freshness. If you have placed yourself in your natural condition, uncontrived freshness, like this, then, at the time when you are free of discursive thoughts, you are seated on the actuality of the mindness and then, when discursive thought proliferates from that, it is the self-occurring luminosity of the dharmakaya. These discursive thoughts do not have to be stopped or furthered; when you rest right on the discursive thought in this way, the discursive thought as such dissolves away into mindness and the dharmakaya itself is there.

That is the way to do the meditation. However, if you just meditate like this once or twice, you will not be able to bring forth the actuality of mind, therefore you have to meditate at all times on the actuality of mind, so that it becomes present like a flowing river.

Now, some people claim that mind actually exists and the outside world is produced by it, and so on; if you think like that, then you have developed a view of permanence. Others claim that there is no mind whatsoever, no karma with cause and effect, and so on; if you think like that, then you have developed a view of nihilism. Abandoning all such ideas, the yogin should always stay in an equipoise of uncontrived freshness.

Now, and as it says in the instruction on the Five Parts, *This ... the definitive meaning of the authentic" should be kept in your heart always. And please, for this that needs no habituation to it; please habituate yourself to it.* So, please keep it in your heart always. Even though there is nothing to be meditated on, please meditate on it again and again. Then it says, *keep impermanence in mind*, so always think of impermanence. Then it says, *always generate a mind of disenchantment*, so always keep the thought in mind that you should gain emancipation from the sufferings of samsara. Then it says, *supplicate the lord.*[112]

Then the text says, *Meditating on Mahamudra like that gets to the point concerning ignorance* meaning that practising Mahamudra like this is the antidote to ignorance; through it, ignorance will collapse. By bringing ignorance to an end, that arises as the wisdom of the dharmadhatu. So the text continues … *will pacify the negative forces of nagas, will bring delusion under control, will liberate from samsara, and causes the wisdom of dharmadhatu to dawn. Therefore, it is important to work assiduously at it*; he said:

> *In the vast open space of mindness,*
> *If there is no assurance in regard to the assembled clouds of*
>   *discursive thought,*
> *The planets and stars of the two knowledges of a buddha will*
>   *not twinkle,*
> *So work assiduously at this non-conceptual mind.*

He says that discursive thoughts are like clouds in the sky; they obscure the two knowledges of buddhahood that are present within us so that they do not shine forth, just as clouds obscure the planets and stars that are present in the sky and prevent their brilliance from shining forth. Unless you build assurance in relation to discursive thoughts[113] the two knowledges of a buddha—the knowledge of things in their depth and things in their extent—will not shine forth, so you must work assiduously at your practice!

---

[112] That is, supplicate the lord guru.

[113] … that is, the assurance of the innate liberation that belongs to discursive thoughts.

When you practise the instructions as given above, you are engaged in path Mahamudra. As you practise the path of Mahamudra and progress, you will pass through what are called the four yogas of Mahamudra, which are four, successive levels of attainment of Mahamudra—they are called The Yoga of One-pointedness, The Yoga of Freedom from Elaboration, The Yoga of One Taste, and The Yoga of Non-Meditation. Roughly speaking, the attainment of the Yoga of One-Pointedness is the attainment of calm-abiding; the attainment of the Yoga of Freedom from Elaboration is the attainment of insight; and the attainment of the remaining two paths is the attainment of increasing levels of unification of calm-abiding and insight. At the end, having completed all of those levels, you will achieve the result of the practice of the path, which is fruition Mahamudra. At that point, you will have completely purified all of the obscurations of mind. At that point, you will have attained the fruition of having practised for your own sake, which is the full manifestation of the dharmakaya and will have attained the fruition of having practised for others' sakes, which is the emanation, for the sake of sentient beings and for as long as samsara exists, of the sambhogakayas and nirmanakayas.

Commentary to the Fifth of the Five Parts, Dedication

"Dedication" means to dedicate all of whatever virtue has been produced through body, speech, and mind to the end that all sentient beings will achieve buddhahood. This is usually done with the recitation of prayers that have been composed for the purpose.

The text says, *The way of making such dedication is that the dedication is done via prajña that sees the emptiness of what is to be dedicated, the dedication, and dedicator.* For someone who has practised meditation on the actuality of mind, the truth of the dharmata, and truly seen it, dedication can be done in the way called dedication with the threefold sphere of emptiness. In it, all three parts of the action of dedication (the virtue dedicated, the act of dedication itself, and the person doing the dedication) are sealed with emptiness, Prajñaparamita. For someone who cannot do that level of dedication, a dedication is done using the words of a prayer. For example:

> Warrior Mañjushri knows how it is,
> And Samantabhadra does too;
> I train following them fully and
> Like them fully dedicate all these virtues.

Thinking that you will make a dedication in the same way as the great bodhisatvas Mañjushri, Samantabhadra, Avalokiteshvara, and so on, repeat the words of the above and that will be sufficient.

You might wonder what will happen if you do not dedicate the merit for the benefit of sentient beings? The conqueror's son Shantideva said:

> Whatever goodness has been accumulated through
> Thousands of aeons by giving, offering to the tathagatas,
> And so on, is destroyed, all of it,
> By a moment of anger.

If we accumulate roots of merit with body, speech, and mind through thousands of aeons—meaning an enormous length of time—but do not dedicate it, then it is said that a moment of any strong affliction—anger, pride, and so on—will cause the virtue to be eliminated. So, the special feature of dedication is that it prevents the roots of merit that we have accumulated from being later destroyed by afflictions.

Moreover, prayers of dedication are the source of great qualities. In the *Sutra Requested by Sagaramati*:

> Just as a drop of water placed into an ocean
> Will not be spent for as long as the ocean is not spent,
> So the roots of virtue dedicated to enlightenment also
> Will not be spent for as long as enlightenment is not
>   obtained.

This uses the example of a drop of water placed into a vast ocean. Just as the drop will remain and not become spent for as long the ocean stays and does not become spent, so the roots of virtue that we dedicate with the attitude of enlightenment mind will stay and not be spent until we have attained enlightenment.

Then Jigten Sumgon said, *Dedication like that gets to the point concerning jealousy* ... meaning that it becomes an antidote for jealousy. As a result, of the five wisdoms, jealousy turns into the all-accomplishing wisdom ... *and causes all-accomplishing wisdom to dawn. Therefore, it is important to work assiduously at that; he said:*

> *If the wish-fulfilling jewel of the two accumulations,*

Is not polished with prayers of aspiration,
The fruit of your wishes will not appear
So work assiduously at the concluding dedication.

Here, he likens the two accumulations—the referential accumulation of merit and the non-referential accumulation of wisdom—to a wish-fulfilling jewel. The jewel needs to be rubbed and polished with vast prayers of aspiration for, if it is not, whatever it is that we want will not come about at all. Therefore, it is important to be work assiduously at making great prayers of aspiration.

Additional Instructions
For Those Who Have Engaged in Practice

People who have found a virtuous spiritual friend or guru and are involved with the practice of meditation need some further instruction. Practitioners will have various afflictions—desire, aggression, pride, and so on—and problems arise so they need instruction on how to bring them to the path of practice.

For the beginner, the methods of the bodhisatva vehicle are an easy way to carry afflictions, sufferings, and so forth onto the path. When very strong afflictions arise, you can think, "Sentient beings have even stronger afflictions than this. Because of it, they accumulate karma and there is no possible end to their wandering in samsara. May all of their afflictions dissolve into the afflictions that I am experiencing now!" Having thought that, develop the certainty, "All of their afflictions have been removed by that!" and then make the prayer "May they go to the level of a sugata!"

That kind of mind can be joined with the "Sending and Taking" practice as follows. On the in-breath, take in all of the afflictions of sentient beings in the form of black smoke and think that it dissolves into yourself. Then, on the out-breath, put all of your virtues together as white light and send it out to all sentient beings; the light dissolves into them to produce all good qualities of mind in them. If you cultivate that over and again, you will be able to turn afflictions that happen to you into the bodhisatva path. There is no difference in the treatment given to any of the five afflictions in this method; they are all treated in the same way.

Sometimes we might become ill. At that time, you can remember that the suffering of pain and sickness of the beings in the lower realms, especially of those in the hell-realms, is far more acute than the pain or discomfort associated with whatever illness you are experiencing. When a genuine feeling of that arises, you can wish that all of their pain and discomfort dissolves into your pain and discomfort and that they are thereby completely relieved of it. If you cultivate that kind of thought, it becomes possible to carry the illness onto the path of enlightenment. For example, it is mentioned in the biography of Khenchen Tashi Ozer that he went to Lhasa at one time and, having arrived there, had some severe head pains. He went to see various people but was not able to cure the illness. Realizing that nothing else could be done, he applied the practice of sending and taking to it and over a period of days the sickness was reduced and finally cleared.

Taken overall, there are different types of illness. One type is of the sort mentioned above; it comes from the full ripening of karma alone and doctors can do nothing to cure it. Another sort is karmic but is based in local conditions, for example, catching a cold due to a change in weather; this can be treated by medication. The first kind, karmic illness, is stated to be of three types in the Tibetan medical system and these correspond to the three main afflictions: wind-related diseases are due to desire, bile-related diseases are due to anger, and phlegm-related diseases are due to delusion. These kinds of sicknesses can be alleviated to a greater or lesser extent by the practices described here of taking adverse circumstances onto the path of enlightenment. That is so because disease comes from the ripening of karmic latencies that have been imprinted on the mind stream by bad deeds done in the past and because the enlightenment mind, which is developed by the Sending and Taking practice, is the very best of methods for overcoming the karmic imprints of bad actions.

The power of the practices of loving kindness, compassion, and enlightenment mind are shown in the following story. Many years ago, the Indian master Asanga went to stay in a mountain cave near Bodhgaya in order to practice the guru-yoga of Maitreya, the coming buddha. After three years, nothing had happened and he became disgruntled and left. As he was leaving, he met an old man who was rubbing an iron rod with a cloth. He asked the man why he would do such a thing. The man replied that he needed a needle and if he polished the iron rod enough, it would eventually wear down to a needle. Asanga was impressed by this display of patience and returned to his cave to meditate again. After another three years, still nothing had happened and he became disgruntled again and left. This time on the way out he saw how birds near the cave had worn down the rocks with the flapping of their wings as they went in and out of their nest. This impressed him again and he returned to his cave once more. After another three years still nothing had happened and he left again. Once again he saw something that impressed on him the need for perseverance and once again he returned to the cave. After another three years, now a total of twelve years, still nothing had happened and this time he left the cave, determined that he was now done with it. When he arrived in a nearby village, he saw a badly under-nourished dog with sores all over its body. The sores were badly infected and maggots were living in them. The dog was almost a corpse. Asanga was overcome with a feeling of compassion for the dog. However, he was equally concerned for the maggots. So he got down on his knees, closed his eyes, and went to gently lick the maggots out of the wounds with his tongue. However, to his surprise, his tongue contacted the ground. He opened his eyes to find that the dog had disappeared and that Maitreya was before him. Asanga asked him where he had been all the time. Maitreya told him that he had been with him right from the beginning, however, due to Asanga's great obscurations produced from former bad actions, Asanga had not been able to see him. Asanga's production of genuine loving kindness and compassion had overcome all of his obscurations and now he could see Maitreya.

At various times we will experience fears, pains, or other difficulties. However, all such things can be successfully dealt with by the one method of bringing it onto the path with enlightenment mind.

❁   ❁   ❁

Glossary of Terms

Actuality, Tib. gnas lugs: A key term in both sūtra and tantra and one of a pair of terms, the other being "apparent reality" (Tib. snang lugs). The two terms are used when determining the reality of a situation. The actuality of any given situation is how (lugs) the situation actuality sits or is present (gnas); the apparent reality is how (lugs) any given situation appears (snang) to an observer. Something could appear in many different ways, depending on the circumstances at the time and on the being perceiving it but, regardless of those circumstances, it will always have its own actuality of how it really is. This term is frequently used in Mahamudra teachings to mean the fundamental reality of any given phenomenon or situation before any deluded mind alters it and makes it appear differently.

Affliction, Skt. kleśha, Tib. nyon mongs: This term is usually translated as emotion or disturbing emotion, etcetera, but the Buddha was very specific about the meaning of this word. When the Buddha referred to the emotions, meaning a movement of mind, he did not refer to them as such but called them "kleśha" in Sanskrit, meaning exactly "affliction". It is a basic part of the Buddhist teaching that emotions afflict beings, giving them problems at the time and causing more problems in the future.

Alaya, Skt. ālaya, Tib. kun gzhi: This term, if translated, is usually translated as all-base or something similar. It is a Sanskrit term that means a range that underlies and forms a basis for something else. In Buddhist teaching, it means a particular level of mind that sits beneath all other levels of mind. However, it is used in several different ways in the Buddhist teaching and changes to a

137

different meaning in each case. In the Mahamudra teachings, an important distinction is made between alaya alone and alaya consciousness.

Alertness, Tib. shes bzhin, samprajana: Alertness is a specific mental event that occurs in dualistic mind. It and another mental event, mindfulness, are the two functions of mind that must be developed in order to develop shamatha or one-pointedness of mind. In that context, mindfulness is what remembers the object of the concentration and holds the mind to it while alertness is the mind watching the situation to ensure that the mindfulness is not lost. If distraction does occur, alertness will know it and will inform the mind to re-establish mindfulness again.

Alteration, altered, same as contrivance q.v.

Assurance, Tib. gdeng: Although often translated as confidence, this term means assurance with all of the extra meaning conveyed by that term. A bird might be confident of its ability to fly but, more than that, it has the assurance that it will not fall to the ground because it knows it has wings and it has the training to use them. Similarly, a person might be confident that he could liberate the afflictions but not be assured of doing so because of lack of training or other causes. However, a person who has accumulated the causes to be able to liberate afflictions is assured of the ability to do so.

Bliss, Skt. sukha, Tib. bde: The Sanskrit term and its Tibetan translation are usually translated into English as "bliss" but refer to the whole range of possibilities of everything on the side of good as opposed to bad. Thus, the term will mean pleasant, happy, good, nice, easy, comfortable, blissful, and so on, depending on context.

Bliss, illumination, and no-thought, Tib. bde gsal mi rtog pa: A person who actually practises meditation will have signs of that practice appear as various types of temporary experience. Most commonly, three types of experience are met with: bliss, illumination, and no-thought. Bliss is an ease of body or mind or both, illumination is the knowing factor of mind, and no-thought is an absence of thought that happens in the mind. The three are usually mentioned when discussing the passing experiences that arise because of practising meditation but there is also a way of describing them as final experiences of realization.

Note that this has often been called "bliss, luminosity, and no-thought" but that makes the mistake that the word for illumination has been abbreviated in this phrase and mistaken to mean something else.

Bodhichitta, Tib. byang chub sems: See under enlightenment mind.

Bodhisatva, Tib. byang chub sems dpa': A bodhisatva is a person who has engendered the bodhichitta, enlightenment mind, and with that as a basis has undertaken the path to the enlightenment of a truly complete buddha specifically for the welfare of other beings. Note that, despite the common appearance of "bodhisattva" in Western books on Buddhism, the Tibetan tradition has steadfastly maintained since the time of the earliest translations that the correct spelling is bodhisatva; see under satva and sattva.

Clinging, Tib. zhen pa: In Buddhism, this term refers specifically to the twofold process of dualistic mind mis-taking things that are not true, not pure, etcetera as true, pure, etcetera and then, because of seeing them as highly desirable even though they are not, attaching itself to or clinging to those things. This type of clinging acts as a kind of glue that keeps a person joined to the unsatisfactory things of samsara because of mistakenly seeing them as desirable.

Concept label, Tib. mtshan ma: This is the technical name for the structures or concepts which function as the words of conceptual mind's language. They are the very basis of operation of the third aggregate and hence of the way that dualistic mind communicates with its world. For example, a table seen in direct visual perception will have no concept labels involved with knowing it. However, when thought becomes involved and there is the thought "table" in an inferential or conceptual perception of the table, the name-tag "table" will be used to reference the table and that name tag is the concept label.

Although we usually reference phenomena via these concepts, the phenomena are not the dualistically referenced things we think of them as being. The actual fact of the phenomena is quite different from the concept labels used to discursively think about them and is known by wisdom rather than concept-based mind. Therefore, this term is often used in Buddhist literature to signify that dualistic samsaric mind is involved rather than non-dualistic wisdom.

Confusion, Tib. 'khrul pa: In Buddhism, this term mostly refers to the fundamental confusion of taking things the wrong way that happens because of fundamental ignorance, although it can also have the more general meaning of having lots of thoughts and being confused about it. In the first case, it is defined like this "Confusion is the appearance to rational mind of something being present when it is not" and refers, for example, to seeing an object, such as a table, as being truly present, when in fact it is present only as mere, interdependent appearance.

Contrivance, contrived, Tib. bcos pa: A term meaning that something has been altered from its native state.

Cyclic existence, Skt. saṃsāra, Tib. 'khor ba: the type of existence that sentient beings have which is that they continue on from one existence to another, always within the enclosure of births that are produced by ignorance and experienced as unsatisfactory.

Dharmakaya, Skt. dharmakāya, Tib. chos sku: In the general teachings of Buddhism, this refers to the mind of a buddha, with "dharma" meaning reality and "kaya" meaning body.

Dharmata, Skt. dharmatā, Tib. chos nyid: This is a general term meaning the inherent property or properties of any given dharma or phenomenon. It can be applied to anything at all. For example, the dharmata of water is its wetness, liquidity, and so on. Dharmata is used frequently in Tibetan Buddhism to mean the most fundamental property of dharmas or phenomena which is their emptiness because of which it is not commonly thought of as meaning "reality". However, that is not correct. To read texts which use this term successfully, one has to understand that the term has a general meaning and then see how that applies in context.

Discursive thought, Skt. vikalpa, Tib. rnam rtog: This means more than just the superficial thought that is heard as a voice in the head. It includes the entirety of conceptual process that arises due to mind contacting any object of any of the senses. The Sanskrit and Tibetan literally mean "(dualistic) thought (that arises from the mind wandering among the) various (superficies *q.v.* perceived in the doors of the senses)".

Elaboration, Skt. prapañca, Tib. spro ba: This is a general name for what is given off by dualistic mind as it goes about its conceptual business. The term is pejorative in that it implies that a story has been made up, un-necessarily, about something which is actually nothing, which is empty. Elaborations, because of what they are, prevent a person from seeing emptiness directly.

Enlightenment mind, Skt. bodhichitta, Tib. byang chub sems: This is a key term of the Great Vehicle. It is the type of mind that is connected not with the lesser enlightenment of an arhat but with the enlightenment of a truly complete buddha. As such, it is a mind which is connected with the aim of bringing all sentient beings to that same level of buddhahood. A person who has engendered this mind has by definition entered the Great Vehicle and is either a bodhisatva or a buddha.

It is important to understand that "enlightenment mind" is used to refer equally to the minds of all levels of bodhisatva on the path to buddhahood and to the mind of a buddha who has completed the path. Therefore, it is not "mind striving for enlightenment" as is so often translated, but "enlightenment mind", meaning that kind of mind which is connected with the full enlightenment of a truly complete buddha and which is present in all those who belong to the Great Vehicle. The term is used in the conventional Great Vehicle and also in the Vajra Vehicle. In the Vajra Vehicle, there are some special uses of the term where substances of the pure aspect of the subtle physical body are understood to be manifestations of enlightenment mind.

Entity, Tib. ngo bo: The entity of something is just exactly what that thing is. In English we would often simply say "thing" rather than entity. However, in Buddhism, "thing" has a very specific meaning rather than the general meaning that it has in English. It has become common to translate this term as "essence" *q.v.* However, in most cases "entity", meaning what a thing is rather than an essence of that thing, is the correct translation for this term.

Equipoise and post-attainment, Tib. mnyam bzhag and rjes thob: Although often called "meditation and post-meditation", the actual term is "equipoise and post-attainment". There is great meaning in the actual wording which is lost by the looser translation.

Essence, Tib. ngo bo: a key term used throughout Buddhist theory. The original in Sanskrit and the term in Tibetan, too, has both meanings of "essence" and "entity". In some situations the term has more the first meaning and in others, the second. For example, when speaking of mind and mind's essence, it is referring to the core or essential part within mind. On the other hand, when speaking of fire or some other thing, there is the entity, fire, and so on, and its characteristics, such as heat, and so on; in this case, it is not an essence but an entity.

Expanse, Skt. dhātu, Tib. dbyings: The Sanskrit term has over twenty meanings. Many of those meanings are also present in the Tibetan equivalent. In the Vajra Vehicle teachings it is used as a replacement for the term emptiness that conveys a non-theoretical sense of the experience of emptiness. When used this way, it has the sense "expanse" because emptiness is experienced as an expanse in which all phenomena appear.

Fictional, Skt. saṃvṛtti, Tib. kun rdzob: This term is paired with the term "superfactual" *q.v.* In the past, these terms have been translated as "relative" and "absolute" respectively, but those translations are nothing like the original terms. These terms are extremely important in the Buddhist teaching so it is very important that they be corrected, but more than that, if the actual meaning of these terms is not presented, then the teaching connected with them cannot be understood.

The Sanskrit term saṃvṛtti means a deliberate invention, a fiction, a hoax. It refers to the mind of ignorance which, because of being obscured and so not seeing suchness, is not true but a fiction. The things that appear to that ignorance are therefore fictional. Nonetheless, the beings who live in this ignorance believe that the things that appear to them through the filter of ignorance are true, are real. Therefore, these beings live in fictional truth.

Fictional and superfactual, Skt. saṃvṛiti, paramārtha: Fictional and superfactual are our greatly improved translations for "relative" and "absolute" respectively. Briefly, the original Sanskrit word for fiction means a deliberately produced *fiction* and refers to the world projected by a mind controlled by ignorance. The original word for superfact means "that *superior fact* that appears on the surface of the mind of a noble one who has transcended samsara" and refers to reality seen as it actually is. Relative and absolute do not convey this meaning at all and, when they are used, the meaning being presented is simply lost.

In more detail, the Sanskrit term behind "fictional", saṃvṛiti, is a common word that was used in ordinary language in India. It means "a fiction", "a deliberate coverup". This word was used in a variety of Indian religions, including Buddhism, to refer to the reality of ordinary beings, ones who are not spiritually advanced. The reality that these beings experience is a trumped up one, a big fiction, made up by their delusion.

The term fictional was paired with another term that was also widely used amongst Indian religions. This other term was used for talking about the reality of beings who are spiritually advanced enough to see things as they really are. The term, "paramartha", means "the spiritually superior (parama) fact known by mind (artha)". This is the fact of how things are. In other words, it refers to the superior level of reality to the fictional one made up by sentient beings, a level which is known by spiritually advanced beings, and which is simply a fact—reality without any fictions. There is no equivalent for this in English so I have coined the new term "superfactual", which is not only a very accurate translation of both the Sanskrit and Tibetan terms but also conveys the meaning correctly, as shown in this paragraph.

The two terms "fictional" and "superfactual" are used in any discussion of the two levels of reality that exist for beings as a whole: the fictional level of reality that sentient beings create for themselves by means of their delusion and the superior, factual level of reality that undeluded beings know as a fact. The terms "relative" and "absolute" sound nice but do not convey either the meanings of the original words nor the meanings that the Buddha gave to them when explaining these two levels of reality. The terms fictional and superfactual not only translate the original terms accurately but also convey the sense of the terms as used by the Buddha. Note the difference in feeling that you get when you use "fictional" and "superfactual" as opposed to relative and absolute.

Fictional truth, Skt. saṃvṛtisatya, Tib. kun rdzob bden pa: See under fictional.

Fictional Truth Enlightenment Mind, Tib. kun rdzob bden pa'i byang chub sems: One of a pair of terms; the other is Superfactual Truth Enlightenment Mind. See under Fictional and Superfactual truth for information about those terms. Enlightenment mind is defined as two types. The fictional type is the conventional type. It is explained as consisting of love and great compassion within the framework of an intention to obtain truly complete enlightenment for the sake of all sentient beings. The superfactual truth type is the ultimate type. It is explained as the enlightenment mind that is directly perceiving emptiness. These explanations belong to the conventional Great Vehicle.

Foremost instruction, Skt. upadeśha, Tib. man ngag: There are several types of instruction mentioned in Buddhist literature: there is the general level of instruction which is the meaning contained in the words of the texts of the tradition; on a more personal and direct level there is oral instruction which has been passed down from teacher to student from the time of the buddha; and on the most profound level there are foremost instructions which are not only oral instructions provided by one's guru but are special, core instructions that come out of personal experience and which convey the teaching concisely and with the full weight of personal experience. Foremost instructions or upadesha are crucial to the Vajra Vehicle because these are the special way of passing on the profound instructions needed for the student's realization.

Great Vehicle, Skt. mahāyāna, Tib. theg pa chen po: The Buddha's teachings as a whole can be summed up into three vehicles where a vehicle is defined as that which can carry a person to a certain destination. The first vehicle, called the Lesser Vehicle, contains the teachings designed to get an individual moving on the spiritual path through showing the unsatisfactory state of samsara and an emancipation from that. However, that path is only concerned with personal emancipation and fails to take account of all of the beings that there are in existence. There used to be eighteen schools of Lesser Vehicle in India but the only one surviving nowadays is the Theravada of south-east Asia. The Greater Vehicle is a step up from that. The Buddha explained that it was great in comparison to the Lesser Vehicle for seven reasons. The first of those is that it is concerned with attaining the truly complete enlightenment of a truly complete buddha for the sake of every sentient being where the Lesser Vehicle is concerned only with a personal liberation that is not truly complete enlightenment and which is achieved only for the sake of that practitioner. The Great Vehicle has two divisions: a conventional form in which the path is taught in a logical, conventional way, and an unconventional form in which the path is taught in a very direct way. This latter vehicle is called the Vajra Vehicle because it takes the innermost, indestructible (vajra) fact of reality of one's own mind as the vehicle to enlightenment.

Ground, Tib. gzhi: This is the first member of the formulation of ground, path, and fruition. Ground, path, and fruition is the way that the teachings of the path of oral instruction belonging to the Vajra Vehicle are presented to students. Ground refers to the basic situation as it is.

Illumination, Skt. vara, Tib. gsal ba: The Tibetan term is an abbreviation of the parent Tibetan term, "'od gsal ba", which is translated with luminosity *q.v.* Illumination is not another factor of mind distinct from luminosity but merely a convenient abbreviation in both Indian and Tibetan dharma language for luminosity.

Introduction and To Introduce, Tib. ngos sprad and ngos sprod pa respectively: This pair of terms is usually mistakenly translated today as "pointing out" and "to point out. The terms are the standard terms used in day to day life for the situation in which one person introduces another person to someone or something. They are the exact same words as our English "introduction" and "to introduce".

In the Vajra Vehicle, these terms are specifically used for the situation in which one person introduces another person to the nature of his own mind. There is a term in Tibetan for "pointing out", but that term is never used for this purpose because in this case no one points out anything. Rather, a person is introduced by another person to a part of himself that he has forgotten about.

Key points, Tib. gnad: it is not apparent from the wording but a "key point" is not a point of understanding that you have conceptually in your mind and take to meditation practice but is an issue belonging to the actual process of meditation itself. Meditation as a process has key points or issues within it and instructions such as the "Three Lines" are given so that the practitioner can connect a correct understanding which is derived from those instructions with those issues as they are actually present in the meditation itself. This is worth thinking over because the common understanding in English of "key point" is an instruction to be applied but that is quite incorrect; the instructions are applied to your meditation in order to work the key points that are present as issues in the meditation itself. They are the buttons existing in the meditation for you to be press using the instructions, such as the Three Lines, that allow you to hit the buttons.

Latency, Skt. vāsanā, Tib. bag chags: The original Sanskrit has the meaning exactly of "latency". The Tibetan term translates that inexactly with "something sitting there (Tib. chags) within the environment of mind (Tib. bag)". Although it has become popular to translate this term into English with "habitual pattern", that is not its meaning. The term refers to a karmic seed that has been imprinted on the mindstream and is present there as a latency, ready and waiting to come into manifestation.

Lesser Vehicle, Skt. hīnayāna, Tib. theg pa dman pa: See under Great Vehicle.

Liveliness, Tib. rtsal: This is a key term in Mahāmudrā. The term is sometimes translated as "display" or "expression" but neither is correct. The primary meaning is the ability of something to express itself but in use, the actual expression of that ability is also included. Thus, in English it would not be "expression" but "expressivity" but that is too dry. This term is not at all dry; it is talking about the life of something and how that life comes into expression; "liveliness" fits the meaning of the original term very well.

Luminosity or illumination, Skt. prabhāsvara, Tib. 'od gsal ba: The core of mind has two aspects: an emptiness factor and a knowing factor. The Buddha and many Indian religious teachers used "luminosity" as a metaphor for the knowing quality of the core of mind. If in English we would say "Mind has a knowing quality", the teachers of ancient India would say, "Mind has an illuminative quality; it is like a source of light which illuminates what it knows".

This term has been translated as "clear light" but that is a mistake that comes from not understanding the etymology of the word. It does not refer to a light that has the quality of clearness (something that makes no sense, actually!) but to the illuminative property which is the nature of the empty mind.

Note also that in both Sanskrit and Tibetan Buddhist literature, this term is frequently abbreviated just to Skt. "vara" and Tib. "gsal ba" with no change of meaning. Unfortunately, this has been thought to be another word and it has then been translated with "clarity", when in fact it is just this term in abbreviation.

Lustre, Tib. mdangs: In both Mahamudra and Great Completion there is the general term "gdangs" meaning what is given off or emitted by something in general, for example the sound given off by a loudspeaker or what the empty factor of mind emits. The Mahamudra teaching makes no difference between that term and this term "mdangs" but the Great Completion teaching does. In Great Completion, this term has the more refined meaning of "lustre" or a subtle output. In this teaching, there is the output of the empty aspect of mind altogether but there is also the lustre of that emptiness.

Maha Ati, Skt. mahāti, Tib. shin tu chen po: Maha Ati or Ati Yoga is the name of the ninth and last of the nine vehicles taught in the Nyingma system of nine vehicles. The name "ati" literally means that it is the vehicle at the end of the sequence of all other vehicles. It is not only the final vehicle at the end of the sequence but the peak of all vehicles given that it presents reality more directly than any of the vehicles below it. It is therefore also called the king of vehicles.

"Mahāsaṅdhi"—"Dzogpa Chenpo" in the Tibetan language and "Great Completion" in the English language—is the name of the teachings on reality contained in the Maha Ati vehicle and also of the reality itself. Great Completion and Maha Ati are often used interchangeably even through their references are slightly different. See Great Completion in the glossary for more.

Manufacture and alteration Tib. bzos bcos: A pair of terms that work together to give the full meaning of leaving something just as it is. The first term of the pair, "construction", means to create something new that was not already there. The second, "alteration", means to make a modification in order to correct something that is already there. Altogether it means neither to create something newly nor to alter what is already there, in other words to leave the situation just as it is, untouched, unmodified.

Mara, Skt. māra, Tib. bdud: The Sanskrit term is closely related to the word "death". Buddha spoke of four classes of extremely negative influences that have the capacity to drag a sentient being deep into samsara. They are the "maras" or "kiss of death" of: having a samsaric set of five skandhas; having afflictions; death itself; and the son of gods, which means being seduced and taken in totally by sensuality.

Migrator, Tib. 'gro ba: Migrator is one of several terms that were commonly used by the Buddha to mean "sentient being". It shows sentient beings from the perspective of their constantly being forced to go here and there from one rebirth to another by the power of karma. They are like flies caught in a jar, constantly buzzing back and forth. The term is often translated using "beings" which is another general term for sentient beings, but doing so loses the meaning entirely. Buddhist authors who know the tradition do not use the word loosely but use it specifically to give the sense of beings who are constantly and helplessly going from one birth to another, and that is how the term should be read. The term "six migrators" refers to the six types of migrators within samsaric existence—hell-beings, pretas, animals, humans, demi-gods, and gods.

Mind, Skt. chitta, Tib. sems: There are several terms for mind in the Buddhist tradition, each with its own, specific meaning. This term is the most general term for the samsaric type of mind. It refers to the type of mind that is produced because of fundamental ignorance of enlightened mind. Whereas the wisdom of enlightened mind lacks all complexity and knows in a non-dualistic way, this mind of un-enlightenment is a very complicated apparatus that only ever knows in a dualistic way.

The Mahamudra teachings use the terms "entity of mind" and "mind's entity" to refer to what this complicated, samsaric mind is at core—the enlightened form of mind.

Mindfulness, Skt. smṛiti, Tib. dran pa: A particular mental event, one that has the ability to keep mind on its object. Together with alertness, it is one of the two causes of developing shamatha. See under alertness for an explanation.

Noble one, Skt. ārya, Tib. 'phags pa: In Buddhism, a noble one is a being who has become spiritually advanced to the point that he has passed beyond samsara. According to the Buddha, the beings in samsara were ordinary beings, spiritual commoners, and the beings who had passed beyond it were special, the nobility.

Output, Tib. gdangs: Output is a general term for that which is given off by something, for example, the sound that comes from a loudspeaker. In Mahamudra and Great Completion, it refers to what is given off by the emptiness factor of the essence of mind. Emptiness is the empty condition of the essence of mind, like space. However, that emptiness has liveliness which comes off the emptiness as compassion and all the other qualities of enlightened mind, and, equally, all the apparatus of dualistic mind. All of this is called its output. Note that the Great Completion teachings have a special word that is a more refined version of this term; see under lustre for that.

Post-attainment: see equipoise.

Prajna, Skt. prajñā, Tib. shes rab: The Sanskrit term, literally meaning "best type of mind" is defined as that which makes correct distinctions between this and that and hence which arrives at correct understanding. It has been translated as "wisdom" but that is not correct because it is, generally speaking, a mental event belonging to dualistic mind where "wisdom" is used to refer to the nondualistic knower of a buddha. Moreover, the main feature of prajña is its ability to distinguish correctly between one thing and another and hence to arrive at a correct understanding.

Preserve, Tib. skyong ba: This term is important in both Mahamudra and Great Completion. In general, it means to defend, protect, nurture, maintain. In the higher tantras it means to keep something just as it is, to nurture that something so that it stays and is not lost. Also, in the higher tantras, it is often used in reference to preserving the state where the state is some particular state of being. Because of this, the phrase "preserve the state" is an important instruction in the higher tantras.

Rational mind, Skt. mati, Tib. blo: Rational mind is one of several terms for mind in Buddhist terminology. It specifically refers to a mind that judges this against that. It is mainly used to refer to samsaric mind, given that samsaric mind only works in the dualistic mode of comparing this versus that. Because of this, the term is mainly used in a pejorative sense to point out samsaric mind as opposed to a non-dualistic enlightened type of mind. However, it is occasionally used to refer to the discriminating wisdom aspect of non-dualistic mind, for example, in the case of a buddha. In that case it is a mind making distinctions between this and that but within the context of non-dualistic wisdom.

This term has been commonly translated simply as "mind" but that fails to identify it properly and leaves it confused with the many other words that are also translated simply as "mind". It is not just another mind but is specifically the sort of mind that creates the situation of this and that (*ratio* in Latin). Therefore, the term "rational mind" fits perfectly. This is a key term which must be understood as a specific term with a specific meaning and should not be just glossed over as "mind".

Realization, Tib. rtogs pa: Realization has a very specific meaning: it refers to correct knowledge that has been gained in such a way that the knowledge does not abate. There are two important points here. Firstly, realization is not absolute. It refers to the removal of obscurations, one at a time. Each time that a practitioner removes an obscuration, he gains a realization because of it. Therefore, there are as many levels of realization as there are obscurations. Maitreya, in the *Ornament of Manifest Realizations*, shows how the removal of the various obscurations that go with each of the three realms of samsaric existence produces realization.

Secondly, realization is stable or, as the Tibetan wording says, "unchanging". As Guru Rinpoche pointed out, "Intellectual knowledge is like a patch, it drops away; experiences on the path are temporary, they evaporate like mist; realization is unchanging".

A special usage of "realization" is found in the Essence Mahamudra and Great Completion teachings. There, realization is the term used to describe what happens at the moment when mindness is actually met during either introduction to or self-recognition of mindness. It is called realization because, in that glimpse, one actually directly sees the innate wisdom mind. The realization has not been stabilized but it is realization.

Rigpa, Tib. rig pa: the key words of key words in the system of the Thorough Cut. The equivalent in the Mahamudra system is "Tha mal gyi shaypa" q.v. Rigpa literally means to know in the sense of "I see!" It is used at all levels of meaning from the coarsest everyday sense of knowing something to the deepest sense of knowing something as presented in the system of Thorough Cut. The system of Thorough Cut uses this term in a very special sense, though it still retains its basic meaning of "to know". To translate it as "awareness" which is common practice these days is a poor practice; there are many kinds of awareness but there is only one rigpa and besides, rigpa is substantially more than just awareness. Since this is such an important term and since it lacks an equivalent in English, I choose not to translate it. However, it will be helpful in reading the text to understanding the meaning as just given.

Samsara, Skt. saṃsāra, Tib. 'khor ba: This is the most general name for the type of existence in which sentient beings live. It refers to the fact that they continue on from one existence to another, always within the enclosure of births that are produced by ignorance and experienced as unsatisfactory. The original Sanskrit means to be constantly going about, here and there. The Tibetan term literally means "cycling", because of which it is frequently translated into English with "cyclic existence" though that is not exactly the meaning of the original Sanskrit term.

Satva and sattva: According to the Tibetan tradition established at the time of the great translation work done at Samye under the watch of Padmasambhava not to mention one hundred and sixty-three of the greatest Buddhist scholars of Sanskrit-speaking India, there is a difference of meaning between the Sanskrit terms "satva" and "sattva", with satva meaning "an heroic kind of being" and "sattva" meaning simply "a being". According to the Tibetan tradition established under the advice of the Indian scholars mentioned above, satva is correct for the words Vajrasatva and bodhisatva, whereas sattva is correct for the words samayasattva, samadhisattva, jñanasattva, and mahasattva and is also used alone to refer to any or all of these three sattvas.

All Tibetan texts produced since the time of the great translations conform to this system and all Tibetan experts agree that this is correct, but Western translators of Tibetan texts have for the last few hundred years claimed that they know better and have changed "satva" to "sattva" in every case, causing confusion amongst Westerners confronted by the correct spellings. Recently, publications by Western Sanskrit scholars have been appearing in which it is admitted that the Tibetan system is and always has been correct.

Secret Mantra, Skt. guhyamantra, Tib. gsang sngags: Another name for the Vajra Vehicle or the tantric teachings.

Seven Points of Vairochana, Tib. rnam par snang mdzad chos bdun: These are the seven aspects of Vairochana's posture, the posture used for formal meditation practice. The posture for the legs is the one called "vajra posture" or vajrasana. In it, the legs are crossed one on top of the other, right on top of left. The advantage of this posture is that, of the five basic winds of the subtle body, the Downward-Clearing Wind is caused to enter the central channel. The posture for the hands is called the equipoise mudra. The right palm is placed on top of the left palm and the two thumbs are just touching, raised up over the palms. The advantage of this posture is that the Fire-Accompanying Wind is caused to enter the central channel. The posture for the spine is that the spine should be held straight. The advantage of this posture is that the Pervader Wind is caused to enter the central channel. The posture for the shoulders is one in which the shoulders are held up slightly in a particular way. The advantage of this posture is that Upward-Moving Wind is caused to enter the central channel. The neck and chin are held in a particular posture: the neck is drawn up a little and the chin slightly hooked in towards the throat. The advantage of this posture is that the Life-Holder Wind is caused to enter the central channel. The tip of the tongue is joined with the forward part of the palate and the jaws are relaxed, with the teeth and lips allowed to sit normally. The eyes are directed down past the tip of the nose, into space. Placing the gaze in this way keeps the clarity of mind and prevents sinking, agitation, and so on.

Shamatha, Skt. śhamatha, Tib. gzhi gnas: This is the name of one of the two main practices of meditation used in the Buddhist system to gain insight into reality. This practice creates a one-pointedness of mind which can then be used as a foundation for development of the insight of the other practice, vipashyana. If the development of shamatha is taken through to completion, the result is a mind that sits stably on its object without any effort and a body which is filled with ease. Altogether, this result of the practice is called "the creation of workability of body and mind".

Six-fold group, Tib. tshogs drug. "Tshogs" means a group, a single collection, and, because of the Sanskrit original, can also simply be a plural-making particle in English. "Tshogs drug" means the six different consciousnesses, taken as a group, of beings in this human realm. There is a second description of the consciousnesses given by the Buddha in which he explains eight consciousnesses, and these taken as one group are correspondingly called "the eight-fold group".

State, Tib. ngang: This is a key term in Mahāmudrā and Great Completion. Unfortunately it is often not translated and in so doing much meaning is lost. Alternatively, it is often translated as "within" which is incorrect. The term means a "state". A state is a certain, ongoing situation. In Buddhist meditation in general, there are various states that a practitioner has to enter and remain in as part of developing the meditation.

Stoppageless, Tib. 'gag pa med pa: This is a key term in Mahamudra and Great Completion. It is usually translated as "unceasing" but this is a different verb. It refers to the situation in which one thing is not being stopped by another thing. It means "not stopped", "without stoppage", "not blocked and prevented by something else" that is, stoppageless. The verb form associated with it is "not stopped" *q.v.* It is used in relation to the practice of luminosity. A stoppageless luminosity is the actual state of reality and what the practitioner has to aim for. At the beginning of the practice, a practitioner's experience of luminosity will usually not be stoppageless but with stoppages.

Superfactual, Skt. paramārtha, Tib. don dam: This term is paired with the term "fictional" *q.v.* In the past, the terms have been translated as "relative" and "absolute", but those translations are nothing like the original terms. These terms are extremely important in the Buddhist teaching so it is very important that their translations be corrected but, more than that, if the actual meaning of these terms is not presented, the teaching connected with them cannot be understood.

The Sanskrit term paramartha literally means "the fact for that which is above all others, special, superior" and refers to what is known to the wisdom mind possessed by those who have developed themselves spiritually to the point of having transcended samsara. That wisdom is *superior* to an ordinary, un-developed person's consciousness and the *facts* that appear on its surface are superior compared to the facts that appear on the ordinary person's consciousness. Therefore, it is superfact or, more colloquially, the highest thing that could be known. What this wisdom knows is true for the beings who have it, therefore what the wisdom sees is superfactual truth.

Superfactual truth, Skt. paramārthasatya, Tib. don dam bden pa: See under superfactual.

Superfice, superficies, Tib. rnam pa: In discussions of mind, a distinction is made between the entity of mind which is a mere knower and the superficial things that appear on its surface and which are known by it. In other words, the superficies are the various things which pass over the surface of mind but which are not mind. Superficies are all the specifics that constitute appearance—for example, the colour white within a moment of visual consciousness, the sound heard within an ear consciousness, and so on.

Suppression and furtherance, Tib. dgag sgrub: Suppression and furtherance is the term used to express the way that dualistic mind approaches the path to enlightenment. In that case, some states of mind are regarded as ones to be discarded, so the practitioner takes the approach of attempting to suppress or stop them, and some are regarded as ones to be developed, so the practitioner takes the approach of trying to go further with and develop them.

These two poles represent the way that dualistic mind always works with itself. Mahamudra practice goes beyond that duality.

Temporary experience, Tib. nyams: The practice of meditation brings with it various experiences that happen simply because of doing meditation. These experiences are temporary experiences and not the final, unchanging experience, of realization.

Tha mal gyi shaypa, Tib. tha mal gyi shes pa: the path term used in the Mahamudra tradition to indicate mind's essence. In Dzogchen, the equivalent term is "rigpa". Both words are used by practitioners as a sort of code word for their own, personal experience of the essence of mind. These words are secret because of the power they are connected and should be kept that way.

Tha mal gyi shaypa is often referred to as "ordinary mind", a term that was established by Chogyam Trungpa Rinpoche for his students. However, there are two problems with that word. Firstly, "tha mal" does not mean "ordinary". It means "common", something that is common to everyone. This is well attested to in the writings of the Kagyu forefathers. Secondly, this is not mind, given that mind is used throughout this book to mean the dualistic mind of beings in samsara. Rather this is "shes pa", the most general term for all kinds of awareness or knower. In short, it is the kind of non-dualistic knower that is common to everyone.

Thorough Cut, Tib. khregs chod: One of the two practices of the innermost level of Great Completion practice. The other is Direct Crossing. Thorough Cut is a practice in which the main point is to cut decisively through to Alpha Purity.

Tirthika, Skt. tīrthika, Tib. mu stegs pa: This is a very kind name adopted by the Buddha for those who did not follow him but who, because they followed some other spiritual path, had at least arrived at the brink of the true path back to enlightenment. The Sanskrit name means "those who have arrived at the steps at the edge of the pool" and comes to mean those on the brink of actually crossing the river of samsara. A lengthy explanation is given in the *Illuminator Tibetan-English Dictionary* by Tony Duff and published by Padma Karpo Translation Committee.

Transparency, Tib. zang thal: perhaps this term would be better not translated. The term is a special term of experience used in both Mahāmudrā and Dzogchen. It means that, because expanse and the knower—described as rigpa in Dzogchen—are unified, there is the experience of total unimpededness. The practitioner is outside the normal constraints of impure appearances and experiences this as a totally open transparency of what is experienced.

Unaltered or uncontrived, Tib. ma bcos pa: the opposite of "altered" and "contrived". Something which has not been altered from its native state; something which has been left just as it is.

Vajra Vehicle, Skt. vajrayana, Tib. rdo rje'i theg pa: See under Great Vehicle.

Vipashyana, Skt. vipaśhyanā, Tib. lhag mthong: This is the Sanskrit name for one of the two main practices of meditation needed in the Buddhist system for gaining insight into reality. The other one, shamatha, keeps the mind focussed while this one looks piercingly into the nature of things.

Wisdom, Skt. jñāna, Tib. ye shes: This is a fruition term that refers to the kind of mind—the kind of knower—possessed by a buddha. Sentient beings do have this kind of knower but it is covered over by a very complex apparatus for knowing, that is, dualistic mind. If they practise the path to buddhahood, they will leave behind their obscuration and return to having this kind of knower.

The Sanskrit term has the sense of knowing in the most simple and immediate way. This sort of knowing is present at the core of every being's mind. Therefore, the Tibetans called it "the particular type of awareness which is there primordially". Because of the Tibetan wording it has often been called "primordial wisdom" in English translations, but that goes too far; it is just "wisdom" in the sense of the most fundamental knowing possible.

Wisdom does not operate in the same way as samsaric mind; it comes about in and of itself without depending on cause and effect. Therefore it is frequently referred to as "self-arising wisdom" q.v.

About the Author,
Padma Karpo Translation Committee,
And Their Supports for Study

I have been encouraged over the years by all of my teachers to pass on the knowledge I have accumulated in a lifetime dedicated to study and practice, primarily in the Tibetan tradition of Buddhism. On the one hand, they have encouraged me to teach. On the other, they are concerned that, while many general books on Buddhism have been and are being published, there are few books that present the actual texts of the tradition. Therefore they, together with a number of major figures in the Buddhist book publishing world, have also encouraged me to translate and publish high quality translations of individual texts of the tradition.

My teachers always remark with great appreciation on the extraordinary amount of teaching that I have heard in this life. It allows for highly informed, accurate translations of a sort not usually seen. Briefly, I spent the 1970's studying, practising, then teaching the Gelugpa system at Chenrezig Institute, Australia, where I was a founding member and also the first Australian to be ordained as a monk in the Tibetan Buddhist tradition. In 1980, I moved to the United States to study at the feet of the Vidyadhara Chogyam Trungpa Rinpoche. I stayed in his Vajradhatu community, now called Shambhala, where I studied and practised all the Karma Kagyu, Nyingma, and Shambhala teachings being presented there and was a senior member of the Nalanda Translation Committee. After the vidyadhara's nirvana, I moved in 1992 to Nepal, where I have been continuously involved with the study, practise, translation, and teaching of the Kagyu system and especially of the Nyingma system of Great Completion. In recent years, I have spent extended times in Tibet with the greatest living Tibetan masters of Great Completion, receiving very pure transmissions of the ultimate levels of this teaching directly in Tibetan and practising them there in retreat. In that way, I have studied and practised extensively not in one Tibetan tradition as is usually done, but in three of the four Tibetan traditions—Gelug, Kagyu, and Nyingma—and also in the Theravada tradition, too.

With that as a basis, I have taken a comprehensive and long term approach to the work of translation. For any language, one first must have the lettering needed to write the language. Therefore, as a member of the Nalanda Translation Committee, I spent some years in the 1980's making Tibetan word-processing software and high-quality Tibetan fonts. After that, reliable lexical works are needed. Therefore, during the 1990's I spent some years writing the *Illuminator Tibetan-English Dictionary* and a set of treatises on Tibetan grammar, preparing a variety of key Tibetan reference works needed for the study and translation of Tibetan Buddhist texts, and giving our Tibetan software the tools needed to translate and research Tibetan texts. During this time, I also translated full-time for various Tibetan gurus and ran the Drukpa Kagyu Heritage Project—at the time the largest project in Asia for the preservation of Tibetan Buddhist texts. With the dictionaries, grammar texts, and specialized software in place, and a wealth of knowledge, I turned my attention in the year 2000 to the translation and publication of important texts of Tibetan Buddhist literature.

Padma Karpo Translation Committee (PKTC) was set up to provide a home for the translation and publication work. The committee focusses on producing books containing the best of Tibetan literature, and, especially, books that meet the needs of practitioners. At the time of writing, PKTC has published a wide range of books that, collectively, make a complete program of study for those practising Tibetan Buddhism, and especially for those interested in the higher tantras. Of them, we especially recommend reading the following texts in conjunction with this book (all published by PKTC and authored by Tony Duff:

- *Gampopa Teaches Essence Mahamudra, Interviews with his Heart Disciples, Dusum Khyenpa and Others*
- *Dusum Khyenpa's Songs and Teachings*
- *The Theory and Practice Of Other Emptiness Taught Through Milarepa's Songs*
- *Samantabhadra's Prayer, Volume I contains a translation and complete explanation of what is also called A King of Aspiration Prayers, Excellent Conduct*
- *The Dzogchen Alchemy of Accomplishment, Heart Guidance on the Practice Expressed in An Easy-to-understand Way*
- *Feature of the Expert, Glorious King*

Digital Resources

PKTC has developed a complete range of electronic tools to facilitate the study and translation of Tibetan texts. For many years now, this software has been a prime resource for Tibetan Buddhist centres throughout the world, including in Tibet itself. It is available through the PKTC web-site.

The wordprocessor TibetDoc has the only complete set of tools for creating, correcting, and formatting Tibetan text according to the norms of the Tibetan language. It can also be used to make texts with mixed Tibetan and English or other languages. Extremely high quality Tibetan fonts, based on the forms of Tibetan calligraphy learned from old masters from pre-Communist Chinese Tibet, are also available. Because of their excellence, these typefaces have achieved a legendary status amongst Tibetans.

TibetDoc is used to prepare digital editions of Tibetan texts in the PKTC text input office in Asia. Tibetan texts are often corrupt so the input texts are carefully corrected prior to distribution. After that, they are made available through the PKTC web-site. These digital editions are not careless productions like so many of the Tibetan texts found on the web, but are highly reliable editions useful to non-scholars and scholars alike. Some of the larger collections of these texts are for purchase, but most are available for free download.

The digital editions can be read, searched, and even made into an electronic library using either TibetDoc or our other software, TibetD Reader. Like TibetDoc, TibetD Reader is advanced software with many capabilities made specifically to meet the needs of reading and researching Tibetan texts. PKTC software is for purchase but we make a free version of TibetD Reader available for free download on the PKTC web-site.

A key feature of TibetDoc and Tibet Reader is that Tibetan terms in texts can be looked up on the spot using PKTC's electronic dictionaries. PKTC also has several electronic dictionaries—some Tibetan-Tibetan and some Tibetan-English—and a number of other reference works. The *Illuminator Tibetan-English Dictionary* is renowned for its completeness and accuracy.

This combination of software, texts, reference works, and dictionaries that work together seamlessly has become famous over the years and has been the basis for many, large publishing projects within the Tibetan Buddhist community around the world.

Index

CPSIA information can be obtained
at www.ICGtesting.com
Printed in the USA
LVHW111219181020
669076LV00003B/775